The Luxury of Afterwards

The Luxury of Afterwards

◆

The Christine Downing Lectures
At San Diego State University
1995–2004

Christine Downing

iUniverse, Inc.
New York Lincoln Shanghai

The Luxury of Afterwards
The Christine Downing Lectures At San Diego State University 1995–2004

iUniverse, Inc.

For information address:
iUniverse, Inc.
2021 Pine Lake Road, Suite 100
Lincoln, NE 68512
www.iuniverse.com

ISBN: 0-595-31086-9

Printed in the United States of America

For Elaine Rother
Without whom, not

Contents

Foreword

Christine Downing's career in the Department of Religious Studies spanned the period from 1974 to 1992, including 13 years as Chair, the publication of numerous articles and books, and a superb teaching record. During the entire time Christine taught here I never once saw her at the national meeting of the American Academy of Religion without a huge stack of blue books under her arm nor did I ever know her to take the three-unit course release time that was due her as department chair. Instead, Chris—the first woman President of the AAR and an internationally recognized scholar who helped transform feminist studies of religion—taught in the trenches with the rest of us.

In 1992, we faced budget cuts similar to those that we face today and, true to form, Professor Downing chose to take a retirement that she did not want in an effort to create future possibilities for the study of religion at San Diego State.

To honor the distinguished career of Professor Downing my predecessor, Irving Alan Sparks, established the annual Christine Downing Lecture. The most whimsical part of Alan's plan to honor Christine came to him several days later—or at least that is how it seemed to the rest of us. Alan came to the faculty and said: "Wouldn't the only thing better than having an annual Christine Downing Lecture be if Christine herself *gave* the lecture?" We readily agreed that this would be a very good thing. Thus, ten more years of intellectual community was born, extending Chris's association with SDSU to a full three decades.

For each of the last ten years, I have told this story as I introduced Chris and each year we laugh again at how this simple plan helped keep our extended family together.

Thank you, Chris, for your uncompromising support of the religious studies program and for this annual celebration of intellectual journeys. You will be sorely missed next spring and each spring after.

Linda Holler, Chair
Department of Religious Studies
San Diego State University

Introduction

A year or so ago as I idly tuned my car radio to PBS, I heard the phrase, "the luxury of afterwards," and immediately knew: *that's* what I'd like to call the gathering together of the "Christine Downing Lectures." I listened more attentively and learned that Allan Gurganus was reading from his best-selling novel, *Oldest Living Confederate Widow Tells All*. Though I have by no means told "all" in these pages, they do serve to give a good sense of the themes and questions that have preoccupied me during the last ten years. I chose the title because it conveys so well the privilege of returning to San Diego year after year and talking about what during that particular year has come to seem most important to talk about—such a different project from teaching one's assigned courses within the department's curriculum. A real luxury, this afterwards, these after-words.

When I retired from San Diego State University in 1992, it was not because I was really ready to, but because, paradoxically, in the context of a catastrophic state budget crisis it seemed the best way to contribute to the ongoing life and vitality of the Department of Religious Studies that I had joined in 1974. What a gift this invitation to return each year to give these lectures has been! I am deeply grateful to Alan Sparks for having the "brilliant" idea and to Linda Holler for its continuing realization. It has meant it wasn't over when it was over. It has made possible staying in touch with beloved colleagues and former students and with that ongoing life: the new faculty, the revised and revisioned curriculum, the new students. It has made possible a gentle weaning. Now there have been ten of these lectures and that seems enough. So: another departure, but one that feels chosen and timely, that incorporates a sense of completion.

Although that 1992 retirement did not, as I initially feared it might, mean the end of my teaching career and I am thoroughly enjoying my present association with Pacifica Graduate Institute in Santa Barbara and believe I am making a real contribution there, my years at San Diego State nevertheless still seem the *central* ones in my professional life. They are, after all, the years in which I wrote all the books I still identify as *my* books, written in *my* voice, about *my* themes. (My earlier writing seems to me, in retrospect, written more by a generic bright young female scholar. That is, of course, an exaggeration but it feels true.) There have been no books since I left—until this one. Thus the dedication of this volume to

Elaine Rother means just what it says—without her shepherding of those books and this one, there haven't been any.

As I look back over the titles of these talks, I am struck by how often I have spoken about memory, about beginnings, about re-visitings—and about re-visioning, the kind of looking forward that looking back makes possible. This suggests to me that this writing has taken place under the aegis of a god I've not consciously honored before: Janus, the god who looks both backward and forward. May he bless us all.

◆   ◆   ◆

Somewhat longer and more formal versions of several of these lectures have appeared elsewhere: in *Soundings,* in *Historical Reflections/Reflexions Historiques,* in *Spring Journal,* and in Dennis Slattery and Lionel Corbett, eds., *Depth Psychology: Meditations in the Field,* and Linda Bennett Elder et al., eds., *Biblical and Humane: A Festschrift for John F. Priest.*

Christine Downing
December 2003

1

Imagination and Memory: Holocaust Reverberations

Indeed, this theme seems to be the principal theme in my life right now, for this January, on the 50th anniversary of the liberation of Auschwitz, I began working on a book whose working title is "Re-Membered Lives." This writing project gives testimony to my belief about the importance of remembering, as the 20th century grows to a close, the events associated with what for me still feels like its defining events: those associated with the years of Nazi rule, the years from 1933 to 1945, the years of the Holocaust, the Shoah.

The book is about remembering—and about the ambivalence that lies behind remembering. Do we remember in order to integrate, to really accept what those events tell us about ourselves? or do we remember in order to at last tie it all up as done? Do we remember in order to remember—or in order to forget?

The events I am pulled to remember no doubt feel more central to me than to most of you—because I am older and thus lived through them, and not only lived through them but had my life decisively shaped by them. I was born in Germany in 1931 and my father was a Jew, at least in Hitler's eyes if not in his own. We left Germany early in 1935 but all my life I have been haunted by the lives I might have led had we not left—one of which would have led me into the Hitler youth, the other to Auschwitz.

And that haunting is what my book will focus on. I know I feel called upon to join those who remember in order not to forget, like the poets whose work Carolyn Forché gathered together in her beautiful book, *Against Forgetting*.

There are three quotations I imagine using as epigraphs.

The first includes some lines from Forché's *Angel of History*

> If a city, ruin.
> If an animal, hunger.
> If a grave, anonymous.
> If a century, this.[1]

The second is from Gaston Bachelard's *Poetics of Reverie*:

> Of childhoods I have so many
> that I would get lost counting them.
> . . . .
> What a lot of beings we have begun!
> What a lot of lost springs which have nevertheless flowed![2]

The third is from Richard Rubenstein's *After Auschwitz:*

> For those of us who lived through the terrible years, whether in safety
> or as victims, the *Shoah* conditions the way we encounter all
> things sacred and profane.[3]

The book expresses my long-held interest in the boundary between imagination and memory—how we are not simply our actual histories but the many intensely imagined possibilities that accompany us as shadow selves. It explores how "I" am "we" and how engagement with these parallel lives makes apparent the interpenetration of past and present, psyche and history. For this engagement with our "other lives" is also an engagement with history, and for me, inescapably, with what Auschwitz reveals about the cruelty and vulnerability of our human being-here. Engaging these sometimes forgotten and now vividly remembered lives is a kind of journey to the underworld, an encounter with the historical reality that is perhaps the most vivid actualization of underworld western history, our history, can provide.

I am convinced of the importance of giving these shadow selves (which I believe all of us to some degree have) a "local habitation and a name," the importance of remembering them in a particularized, detailed way and thus re-member-ing myself. Such remembering is an act of soul not intellect—a regathering of lost possibilities.

My interest in *imagined* earlier lives is in part inspired by Gaston Bachelard's "Reveries Toward Childhood" in which he writes of how part of our ongoing lives consists of the possibilities open in childhood that were never literally lived—but which nonetheless accompany us as shadows, as parallel lives. For Bachelard these alternate lives seem to be mostly concerned with happiness, fulfillment. For me they involve more fearsome possibilities.

Because I view such remembering as an act of creative imagination, another important model has been "The Three Lives" or "Three Incarnations" included as an Appendix to Hermann Hesse's *Magister Ludi.* These three "Lives" are presented as composed by the novel's protagonist, Joseph Knecht, during the last phase of his initiation, a period during which the only obligation is that each year the students of Castalia compose a fictitious autobiography in which they imagine themselves transposed back into some period of the past. Although what happens to these heroes is very different from what happens in Knecht's own life, though there are no neat analogical, allegorical parallels, we do recognize, "Yes; this *is* the same person." Although Knecht did not literally believe in these past lives, he felt he knew himself better for having imagined them. Knecht's other lives were set in a different time and place, were "wish-dreams;" whereas mine are not past but parallel lives and perhaps more "fear-dreams" than "wish-dreams."

A few years ago I read Alan Lightman's *Einstein's Dreams*, a fictional account of Einstein's discovery of the theory of relativity, which imagines Einstein dreaming of the many different kinds of time that might exist. One, he eventually decides, represents the kind of time that exists in *our* world. Not that others are impossible. Time might work differently in other worlds. In one of these worlds a man is deciding whether to visit a woman who lives in Freiburg. He decides not to see her again and his life unfolds in a particular way; three years later he meets another woman with whom he lives happily. He decides that he must see her again; they begin a conflict-filled relationship; he lives for her and is happy with his anguish. He also decides that he must see her again; he goes to her house; after an hour she says she must go to help a friend; they say goodbye; he goes home. "These three chains of events all indeed happen, simultaneously. For in this world, time has three dimensions, like space. Each future moves in a different direction of time. Each future is real. At every point of decision, the world splits into three worlds, each with the same people but with different fates for these people."[4]

There is a sense in which I believe that this is how time operates in our world, in my world, in the world of poetry, in the world of the soul.

I know I want my book to honor the impact of historical events on us, on our inner lives, our sense of self, our souls, as Christa Wolf's *Kindheitsmuster* (translated both as *Patterns Of Childhood* and as *A Model Childhood*) so powerfully does. In this book Wolf (who was born just two years before me in a small town in eastern Germany that is now in Poland) writes of her first trip back to that town decades later and all the long forgotten, indeed repressed, memories of a childhood in Hitler's Germany it stirred up. She was joined by her three year younger brother, by her husband and their daughter, who was then the age Wolf had been in 1945 when she and her family fled from the advancing Russian army (and who can't understand the point of the trip nor why she had to be included). Part of what fascinates me about the book is what Wolf has to say about how she had to struggle to find the right form for the writing. She ends up using a different name for her childhood self, Nelly, and writes about her in the third person, as "she." She writes of present self in the second person, as "you." She leaves it open how much in her account of her early years is remembered, how much invented. "None [of the characters in the book] is *identical* with any person living or dead. Neither do any of the described episodes *coincide* with actual events." She acknowledges wanting to reject, disown this child self. She writes of the difficulties she experienced in writing, the many delays between finishing one chapter and beginning the next and the pain of having to uncover her many strategies of concealment, the hypocrisy of attempting to use 'her' for a confrontation with the self. "Do you imagine that you can understand someone of whom you're ashamed? Whom you defend, whom you misuse in order to defend yourself?" Even though (like me) she was much too young to have been either a hero or perpetrator, she sees now how the all-pervasive Nazi got inside and destroyed her sense of self. She writes of how unbearable it is "to think the tiny word 'I' in connection with the word 'Auschwitz.' 'I' in the past conditional: I would have. I might have. I could have. Done it. Obeyed orders." At the end of the book, she wonders:

> The child who was hidden from me—has she come forth? Or has she been scared into looking for a deeper, more inaccessible hiding place? Has memory done its duty? Or has it proven—by the act of misleading—that it's impossible to escape the mortal sin of our time—the desire not to come to grips with oneself? And the past, which can still split the first person into the second and the third—has its hegemony been broken? Will the voices be still?
>
> I don't know.[5]

The impulse to undertake my engagement with my shadow selves was triggered by a similar journey, a trip back in September 1992 to Saxony, the homeland to which I'd never before returned since I left when I was four (though I'd been back many times to western Germany). My experience of this trip back was, of course, colored by what I had just been going through in my present life: the sudden loss of my own professorial position here at SDSU which in some eerie (though admittedly small scale) ways echoed my father's experience of losing his job at the University of Leipzig sixty years earlier, and the death of my dearest friends to AIDS, a plague which in some ways is also a "holocaust."

It took a while for the impact of the trip to assume the shape of this project. What I was at first most aware of was that no new childhood memories had been evoked during those days spent in the city where I and my parents had lived during my first few years or in the smaller towns where my parents grew up between which I was shuttled during my last year in Germany when we no longer had a home of our own. What was new was a profound sense of how *young* my parents had been when their whole world fell apart, younger than any of my own children now were.

As I have already noted, I was born in Germany in 1931. My father was half Jewish by birth though Lutheran in upbringing; my mother's family was staunchly Lutheran. My father, a university professor, lost his job in 1933, a few months before my brother was born. In November 1934, after fruitless attempts to find a position as a chemist in Germany, he came to America; by then my mother was already pregnant with their third child. Three months after my sister's birth, my mother and we three children joined my father in America. We arrived on the Fourth of July.

All my life, as I have also already noted, I have been haunted by two alternate lives I might so easily have lived. One of these is the life that would have unfolded had my entire family stayed in Germany and eventually been sent to an extermination camp.

The other is connected to the possibility that my gentile mother might have agreed to the urgings of both sets of grandparents and decided not to follow my father to America. The force of these urgings is suggested by the fact that her father—and she was very much a father's daughter—never forgave her for choosing to go to America (as he'd almost not forgiven her for marrying a man he viewed as a Jew) and never had any further contact with her. As I have long imagined this possibility, my parents would have been divorced, my mother would have returned to the small town where her father had been the headmaster of the most prestigious boys' secondary school and eventually have married the childhood sweetheart who was still in love with her. (She still talks today, in her nineties, of this young man who used to walk her home from dancing school and who later, when they were both adults, contacted my mother as soon as he learned of what had happened to my father to ask her if there was anything he might do to help.) I would have grown up absorbing the taken-for-granted anti-Semitism of that milieu and very likely the Nazi enthusiasms of my peers (like Christa Wolf).

These two other selves have always been there for me, though obviously during my first few years in America there was more just a sense of "the girl I left behind in Germany," the girl who would go on with her/my life there, the girl who still saw her grandparents regularly, the girl who still spoke our mother tongue. Especially at first she, her life, felt even more real than the life of the one who had suddenly found herself uprooted. I can remember dreaming of her every night, keeping her alive.

Only gradually did she become two, as I only gradually discovered that I was partly Jewish by birth and that we had left Germany because of that, and as I only gradually learned how much the life of a German Jewish girl would differ from that of a gentile peer. My given name was Christine Rosenblatt: an obvious sign of this double destiny to those who could read such signs. But I can still remember vividly the occasion when I was ten years old when for the first time a stranger, hearing my name, let me know she assumed I was Jewish, and how disbelieving I was.

Since then they have always been there, these two other selves, haunting my dreams, shaping my feelings, affecting my decisions in ways only recognized retrospectively. I have come to sense how they have helped determine whom I've chosen as friends, how they've entered into my scholarly involvements with Buber and Freud (who in a sense are the Jewish grandfathers I never knew) how my most basic sense of what the world is like is due more to them than to anything I've experienced in my protected life here in America. I remember how important it was to me to take my children while they were all still in elementary school to Germany for a year, because of my sense that only then could they know who I am. (As it turned out we were there in the spring of 1968, at the very time that young Germans rose up to protest their elders' amnesia about the Hitler years.)

They have always been there, these two other selves, but as vague presences, never quite in focus, never directly engaged. I think this is partly because my family sought in so many ways to act as though our real life began in 1935, began in America. My father has never thought of himself as Jewish, felt he, not Hitler, knew who he truly was, and so never talked about our leaving Germany because of his having been identified by the Nazis as a Jew. He refused ever to set foot in Germany again until in 1972 he agreed to return for a 50th secondary school reunion. Since then the friends of his youth have again played an important role in his life. Yet these re-established friendships clearly depend on a bracketing of the Nazi years—just the years I need to confront.

About ten years ago I had a dream in which I was a half-breed Native American youth called upon by the elders of my tribe to serve as the Keeper of the Tribe's Symbols and Lore. I resisted because I felt I had not been raised within the tribe but eventually yielded to the elders' sustained persuasion. I understood the dream then in a way that had relevance to my life then. Now I see it as a dream calling me (whom the Nazis classified as a *Mischling,* a crossbreed, a mongrel) to *this* task.

I have been struck as I've begun to immerse myself in memoirs of the Nazi period how for so many others, who lived my imagined lives more literally, the need to look at that time, those events, has become urgent only now, in the last few years. Perhaps the immediate need after the war was to go on with one's life, setting aside this period as an encapsulated other time and to devote all one's conscious energies to *living.* Now that children have been raised and careers brought to a close, it becomes important to dissolve that protective shell and to create a version of one's life that includes that time.

I have more and more recognized the truth of Elie Wiesel's observation that collective experience lies behind every memoir. Although in some sense I will be writing *fiction,* it has been evident to me that I cannot base my writing simply on personal memory and imagination, for I want a kind of "verisimilitude" that requires a grounding in the history of the period and an immersion in others' accounts of their experiences during it.

I also know that what I'm after is not an engagement with the villain/victim archetype or with a simplistic polarization of cruelty and vulnerability. These other lives that I want to see more clearly are not simply the stereotypes, the beautiful female Aryan SS Kommandant or the Jewish girl sent directly to the gas chamber at Auschwitz. I want somehow to know, to be able to imagine clearly, what really might have happened—and this requires learning more than I already knew about the details of the Nazi years in Germany. This has meant recognizing that there are actually multiple possible other lives: we might have left for Holland rather than America and found ourselves back under Nazi rule in 1940 (like Anne Frank's family) or I might have been sent to a foster family in England, or…or…Historically, there were many alternatives. Indeed, my reading has taught me that ending up at Auschwitz or another extermination camp was a much less likely possibility (for me, a German second degree *Mischling*) than I had previously always imagined. Which, however, doesn't change that it is this possibility that is alive for me. What I'm interested in are these *two* alternate lives that have haunted me, but that I now need to see in a more particularized, more precisely imagined way.

My grand-daughters to whom I imagine dedicating this book have helped me re-imagine myself when I was a young girl. Watching them grow up has helped me see the four year old I was when we left Germany, the seven year old I would have been at the time of *Kristallnacht,* after which German Jewish children were barred from German schools, the nine year old I would have been when the German Jews were deported to ghettos in Poland or to Terezin, the 11 or 12 year old I might have been when those Jews were sent on to extermination camps like the one at Auschwitz.

As I first began to envision this book, I saw it as having *four* parts. The first would cover the years from 1900 to 1935 and recounts the family history and personal history that the I who went to America share with these other two selves. I want to include my version of my parents' lives during the first third of this century, a century which for me begins with the publication of Freud's *Interpretation of Dreams* in 1900, and my father's birth in 1901. I have had a much more vivid sense of my parents' early lives since my trip back to the towns in which they grew up which made me so aware of how young they were in the 1930s. My parents had waited six years to get married while my father finished his doctoral degree and began a professorial appointment in the same department at the University of Leipzig as Werner Heisenberg and Edward Teller. Almost exactly a year after their wedding, I was born. The life they had dreamt of was just beginning to become fact. My mother turned thirty on February 28—the day after the Reichstag Fire, the day of the legalization of arbitrary imprisonment, the day Thomas Mann away on a lecture tour was told by his children to stay in Switzerland, that it wouldn't be safe to return to Germany. Three weeks later, on my second birthday, the first concentration camp, the one at Dachau, opened. By early May Freud's books had been burned and my father had lost his job. In July my brother, conceived when the future still seemed so full of promise, was born. A year later my father, unable to find any work as a chemist in Germany, was on his way to America. My mother, pregnant with their third child, and we two little ones stayed behind, living alternatively with the two sets of grandparents—both of whom (for quite different reasons) urged her to have an abortion and to stay in Germany rather than to join her husband in America. She resisted and a few months after my sister's birth, we came. As I look now at photographs of my mother in those first years here I see her looking so painfully depressed and can't help wondering: would it have been easier for her to have stayed?

Even as I narrate this all too brief a summary, I recognize anew the ethical issues that arise because in telling one's own story, one is telling other people's as well. I know how important it would be to communicate that I know that in some sense these are "my characters," that my parents themselves, or my siblings, for example, would tell these stories differently.

The second part of my book, as I conceived it, would consist of an account of the relevant aspects of the life of the me who went to America—which would begin in 1935 and perhaps go on to 1952 when, pregnant with my first child, I made my first return visit to Germany and stayed with the man whom I imagine my mother might have married had she stayed. This me would have to be included in part because the other me's, as I imagine them, would not be generic gentile or Jewish German girls of my generation, but *me,* with my particular quirks, gifts and weaknesses. To write this part of the story, to help me imagine *this* self, I have available an autobiography I wrote when I was in the eighth grade.

To help me imagine the me whom I in shorthand think of as "the German girl" I have not only read all the relevant books I could find (among which those by Christa Wolf and Carola Stern seem most pertinent) but also wrote to two cousins (both *Mischlings* like myself) who stayed in Germany outside the camps and told them what I was up to. Their many-paged responses were fascinating and very moving. They made me feel I was undertaking this project for them as well as for myself.

To help me imagine the me whom I think of as "the Jewish girl" I have immersed myself in Holocaust history and fiction, especially in memoirs, especially the memoirs of females, and most particularly the memoirs of those who were about my age. This has issued in some strangely compelling *recognitions.* When I visited the Jewish cemetery in Prague, I for the first time saw the drawings and poems composed in the Nazi camp at Terezin by girls just my age. This led us to stop at this camp on our way to Dresden. Somehow I knew immediately I was *there.* So I have read a lot about that particular camp (the one to which Freud's sisters were sent) and have found especially evocative Arnold Lustig's descriptions of the interactions among the children who were interned there.

My reading has made me aware of many problematics involved in writing about the Holocaust. Some authors, emphasizing its "sacrality," see it as a unique event whose horror must not be diminished. They see focusing on the "everyday-ness" aspects of living through this period as "normalizing" the Holocaust, and thus inserting it as a too easily assimilable event in the course of ongoing history.

Others insist the Holocaust should not be rendered unique in a way that isolates it and so prevents it from touching our lives in the present. Some see any fictional treatment of the Holocaust as something that dangerously supports those who deny its literal historicity. There are those who regard any artistic reshaping of the "facts" as something that puts the emphasis on the writer's subjectivity, on his or her *persona* or esthetic powers rather than on the universal significance of what happened.

No wonder I sometimes experience fear and often feel uncertainty about how to actually *do* this.

Beyond the more particular questions there's the whole issue of whether one has the right to tell the story at all. Not so much Theodor Adorno's question as to whether the Holocaust *can* be written of, but more Elie Wiesel's assertion that only those who actually lived it can say what it was like. Yet Wiesel also says "anyone who does not actively, constantly engage in remembering and making others remember, is an accomplice of the enemy."

And there is a very real sense in which I, too, *am* a survivor.

A sense in which I feel that these other selves are using me, are calling on me to remember them, to be their witness.

There are so many books already, so many memoirs—*and yet only I can tell* this story.

These considerations have already led me to re-imagine the form of my book, to see it differently than I did at first.

I now imagine beginning thus: "*That* dream again…the one where I find myself going in search of HER and make my way to an underground cave where I clearly sense HER presence and yet find myself unable to see her." For I see that this dream (which originally led me to the goddesses of ancient Greece and then to my sister and sisterly others) is one I now understand as calling me to go in search of these two alternate selves.

And whereas I had at first imagined writing fictional accounts of these lives on Hesse's model I now think I must rather imagine myself in the process of trying to get them into focus—much as I might try to pull back into consciousness an evanescent dream. So I think I need to address each (somewhat as in Gestalt therapy one might address a silent figure in the other chair) with my questions, my imaginings. For each SHE can tell her story only in dialogue with me, for in a sense SHE exists only in that dialogue, has no existence apart from our interaction. (I wonder also if "I" might have some meaning for THEM? as a fantasy other who left?) I see that the "I" that wants to know them inevitably knows some things about their lives they *couldn't* know, *because* I know the wider context within which their individual experiences took place, a context inaccessible to anyone then.

As I imagine trying to call these two shadow selves forth by name, I realize that neither could have continued to go by my name, Christine Rosenblatt. The last name would have been much too blatantly Jewish to have protected me as "the German girl," the first name too Christian for a girl now identified with her Jewishness. So to contact the first I would have to address her as "Christine Fischer Tollert;" she would retain "my" first name, have my mother's maiden name as a middle name, and the last name of my mother's childhood sweetheart (the man I imagine my mother might have remarried) as a last name. Thus the Jewish part of her heritage would have to all intents and purposes been erased—so thoroughly that she herself would have no knowledge of it.

At first I thought I might call the other shadow self Tina (as I was often called as a child) or Sara (as by Nazi orders all Jewish females had to be called)—but at some point I *knew* her name was Ruth, in tribute to the biblical Ruth who said so staunchly, "Where you go, there will I go...."

It has also become clear to me that instead of trying to put together a neatly ordered chronological account, I will rather proceed along associational patterns, with an emphasis on epiphanies, paradigmatic moments. I want to avoid the kind of coherence, of teleological emplotment, that narrative patterns, "secondary elaboration," encourage. In comparing the form of spontaneous oral testimonies with that of the more consciously shaped written memoirs, Lawrence Langer has found that for survivors the past lives in the present only in disjoined form; I feel this is how it lives in my psyche, too.

I also "know" that both these SHEs had died by the end of the war, one at Auschwitz, the other perhaps in the firebombing of Dresden (through which one of my grandmothers actually lived). I have always assumed that I would have died (as almost all did)—though I don't imagine myself as essentially different from those who did.

'I' (the "American girl") am the survivor not these SHEs, these shadows who accompany me. For me these SHEs only exist *then*, not before or after.

Any "after" for them would, as I imagine it, not be all that different from my own "after." (I was amazed by a photo in the memoir written by Anne Frank's stepsister who unlike Anne survived Bergen-Belsen and Auschwitz: the photo shows her at her wedding the year I, too, was married; her wedding suit looks identical to mine.)

I still vividly remember asking a German youth only a year or two older than I whom I met when I first went back to Germany in 1952 what I should do with my life in the light of all the horrors that I had escaped. "Live in a way that shows it is still possible to live an ordinary happy life," he answered. In trying to do that these last forty years or so, I believe I have in a sense lived the "future" of all three of these alternate selves.

Writing this book feels so important to me, and yet I find myself still preparing, avoiding, waiting. I don't really know what I'll find or how it will affect me. Some kind of truth about me, about the multiple selves I am, about the interpenetration of past and present, psyche and history, the conscious and the unconscious, the metaphorical and the literal. There is a sense in which I already know all this, and a more important sense in which I don't.

My hope is not to assimilate or erase these shadow selves—but to honor the role they play in my life. In some sense this writing is grief-work but it is not exorcism. I had expected to be writing a quite different book now, one based on the Orpheus-Eurydice mythologem, on the theme of male and female journeys to the underworld. I see how this book is connected to that one—how the point is not to rescue the two shadow selves who live in the "underworld" but to attend to their experience there. I see myself as like an Orpheus who goes to the underworld to make contact with a lost one (or rather two) but knows that I have to leave them there, that they belong there.

In a sense this book is not so much a "Holocaust book" as it is a book about the co-presence of various lives, the *reality* of alternate lives not literally lived. It is a book about *re-membering* AND about *still being dis-membered.*

But in another sense the book *is* an attempt to understand the 20th century in relation to the Holocaust as its defining moment. For although it may be true that as someone who would only have been 14 even at the end of World War Two I could not have been a perpetrator or in any very significant way even a bystander (and might very well historically not even have been a victim in the full-on, murdered at Auschwitz sense)—that is not true of me as an almost seventy year old woman at the end of the century. This "she" hopes this looking back might help me live more consciously and responsibly now—which means not living as a bystander in the face of our present world's challenges and horrors.

Notes

1. Carolyn Forché, *The Angel of History* (New York: HarperCollins, 1994) 6.

2. Gaston Bachelard, *The Poetics of Reverie* (Boston: Beacon, 1971) 112.

3. Richard L. Rubenstein, *After Auschwitz,* 2nd ed. (Baltimore: The Johns Hopkins University Press, 1992) 200.

4. Alan Lightman, *Einstein's Dream* (New York: Pantheon, 1993) 18–22.

5. Christa Wolf, *A Model Childhood* (New York: Farrar, Straus and Giroux, 1980) 1 (my italics) 211, 230, 406.

2

How Little It Resembles Memory: The Book of Ruth— Its Biblical Context, Its Contemporary Meanings

My talk this year is in some ways a continuation of the one I gave last year in which I spoke of my current major writing project, one which I have still not completed. I spoke of how I was born in Germany in 1931 to a father who was a Jew, at least in Hitler's eyes. And of how because he was a university professor, my father lost his job in 1933 when Hitler came to power, and how by 1935 my family had resettled in America. So we left early, long before Auschwitz.

Yet all my life I have been haunted by a shadow self, the life I would have led had my family not left, a life that would have ended in one of the extermination camps. She, this other self, has always been there, haunting my dreams, shaping my feelings, affecting my decisions in ways only recognized retrospectively—but as a vague presence, never quite in focus, never directly engaged. But, as I said last year, it has now become time for me to get this shadow self, this self that still lives in the shadows, in focus. I need to see her more clearly—in order to see myself clearly.

I had at first imagined writing a fictional account of her life but came to realize I must rather imagine myself in the process of trying to get her into focus, much as I might try to pull back into consciousness an evanescent dream. I needed to address her (somewhat as in Gestalt therapy one might address a silent figure in the other chair) with my questions, my imaginings.

But to engage her in dialogue I need to call her forth by name, and it seems obvious to me that it would not be Christine Rosenblatt. The girl who went to Terezin with her father, because of her Jewish roots, and eventually to Auschwitz would not have stayed Christine. At first I thought she might have become

14

known as Sara, the name the Nazis required all Jewish females to adopt. But then suddenly I knew—she would have been called Ruth.

My reading these last few years has taught me that actually, historically, ending up in an extermination camp was a much less likely possibility for me, a second degree *Mischling* according to the Nuremberg Laws, than I had previously always imagined. But nevertheless that is the alternate life that had always haunted me, because a part of me has always felt with respect to my Jewish ancestry, whither thou goest, I will go.

I know that, born of a non-Jewish mother and never inculcated in Jewish ritual, in Jewish eyes I am not a Jew at all. Yet, since I first became aware of my family history I have always felt a strong connection to my Jewish heritage—to the stories not to the religion, to the people not to the god.

As most of you know I have devoted much of my time in the last few decades to the stories of ancient Greece and to contemporary, especially feminist, rereadings of these stories. But the Hebrew stories are mine, too. I keep returning to them, to Sara and Abraham, to Esau and Jacob, to Rachel and Leah, to Tamar, to Joseph—to Ruth.

And for the last year, ever since I knew that I would use the name Ruth to call forth the story of this hidden other self, I have found myself involved with the biblical book in which she appears—diverted from my "real" writing project—with no idea really how much if any of this will be part of the book I'm still working on. But in some way having to do this first. Having to get that Ruth in focus, having to discover what relevance her story might have to mine.

This has happened before. This unanticipated pull to the Hebrew Bible. When I began work on my doctoral dissertation on Martin Buber I had imagined focusing on Buber's philosophy of dialogue but found myself instead giving equal prominence to his translation of the Hebrew Bible into German and to his biblical commentaries.

When I first started teaching in 1963, I was required to teach Hebrew Scriptures even though I had never had a course in it—and found I loved doing so.

When I returned from my first sabbatical in the fall of 1968 and discovered that during my year away my students had suddenly become feminists, it was in this course, with respect to these texts, that these students first forced me to see anew—with feminist eyes.

But then in 1974 I came to SDSU and never again had a chance to teach these texts, these stories I had come to love, since we had Yitz Gefter, a trained specialist, here on our faculty to do so. (Though I did once sneak in a whole semester on the biblical book of Genesis and Thomas Mann's reworkings of the Genesis stories in his *Joseph and His Brothers* in a course on Religion and Literature.)

So perhaps this is my revenge—taking this opportunity to at last to talk for a while on this campus about a biblical text—the Book of Ruth.

It is a timely book to talk about at this time of year, between Passover and Shavuot (which will fall on May 23 this year)—in the middle of the 50 day interval between the traditional beginning of the barley harvest and the end of the wheat harvest, the period during which most of the activity in the Book of Ruth takes place.

I remember being taught that in Greece the stories belonged to the poets, and that the poets kept the myths alive through their creative reworking of them. In Israel, by contrast, I was told, the stories belonged to the priests, who held that there was only one right way to tell them, the way enshrined in the canon.

But, of course, this isn't true, at least not for Jews. Torah and midrash belong together. According to the sages there is always another interpretation, always another way of telling or understanding the tale, and all later commentary, not just the commentary of the Talmudic or medieval rabbis but our commentary too, is implicit in the revelation given at Sinai, as though already written in invisible ink. Midrash, as Jacob Neusner tells us, writes *with* Scripture rather than *about* it.

Midrash immerses us in a sea of quotations, allusions, elaborations, extrapolations, and plausible inventions; it adds ethical judgment, sociological density, and psychological motivation to biblical texts. To engage in midrash is to look at what's troubling in a biblical text, to note contradictions, missing details. Midrash gives us fresh, passionate, playful rereadings of the Torah which honor, challenge, and sometimes subvert the traditional tales.

Midrash assumes intertextuality; it assumes that each text in the Bible can only be fully understood when brought into connection with all the others, with the redacted whole. Which makes me think of how Freud said that to fully follow the thread of associations evoked by a single dream would yield a whole life—and of how I have learned that to adequately tell a single Greek myth would lead one to tell all the other stories that comprise Greek mythology—not that one ever can follow all of those associations, tell all those other stories…

I have been amazed as I have read the midrashic responses of medieval rabbis to the Book of Ruth how they seem to find questions to raise about every verse, how passionately they disagree, how farfetched some of their associations are. No more (or less) farfetched, I'd say, than some of my own associations.

As you may have guessed, the midrashic versions of the biblical stories which I love most are those to be found in Thomas Mann's *Joseph and His Brothers*. But Mann never wrote about Ruth, and it is Ruth who has become focal for me. Ruth, whose connection to the Jewish story was peripheral, easily disowned, until she chose to make it central. It's her choice of a destiny that moves me—and also that she made her choice on the basis of her commitment to a woman.

For even though in my own case the shadow self that might have gone to Auschwitz would have followed her father there, nevertheless part of the power of this story for me is the way in which it is a story about a woman's love for a woman. What first draws us to a story is not always what keeps us returning to it.

Of course, one returns to a story for many different reasons. I've been struck by how many contemporary women, particularly Jewish women, are pulled to reclaim this story as their own. How as adults they discover depths and complexities in the story that they had not been aware of when they heard it as children.[1]

The title for my talk this afternoon, "How Little It Resembles Memory," comes from a poem, "The Book of Ruth and Naomi," by Marge Piercy:

> When you pick up the Tanakh and read
> the Book of Ruth, it is a shock
> how little it resembles memory.
> It's concerned with inheritance,
> lands, men's names, how women
> must wiggle and wobble to live.
>
> Yet women have kept it dear
> for the beloved elder who
> cherished Ruth, more friend than
> daughter. Daughters leave. Ruth
> brought even the baby she made
> with Boaz home as a gift.
>
> Where you go, I will go too,
> your people shall be my people,
> I will be a Jew for you,
> for what is yours I will love
> as I love you, oh Naomi
> my mother, my sister, my heart.[2]

The Book of Ruth reads like a folktale, like the legends in Genesis, and its focus on food and famine, on infertility and birth, suggest it might once (as part of a lost oral tradition) even have been connected to some old goddess tale. Gunkel suggested a parallel to the Egyptian myth of Isis and Osiris, in which the widowed Isis manages magically to conceive a legitimate heir even though her husband is dead. Many scholars think it may originally have been a tale told or sung by women, like the Songs of Miriam and Deborah.

Unlike most biblical stories, God is only peripherally involved in the action of the story—though he is said to have brought an end to the famine in Bethlehem and at the end of the story to have given Ruth conception, and there is a hint that it is not really simply by chance that it is Boaz's field to which Ruth goes to glean. As Jacob Neusner suggests, that seems to be part of the point of the story: that it is in the events of everyday village life that God is present.

But though it is very likely based on an old folktale and appears at first reading to be such a simple, artless short tale, as part of my own adult return to this text, I have come to appreciate what an artfully constructed composition this little story is. Note, for example, the shifts of pace, the suspense-creating foreshadowing, the symmetries between the first and fourth chapters and between the second and third.

I have discovered that actually it is a sophisticated, perhaps deliberately anachronistic, composition, with clearly intended, pointedly meaningful, allusions to other biblical texts, which was probably written in the post-exilic period—that is, very late, as Biblical texts go. Probably but by no means certainly—it is amazing how many disagreements there are about this simple story—about when it was written or about why it's in the Bible at all.

Certainly I have found much in this story as I turn to it now—drawn in by that name, Ruth, which leads me to agree: "how little it resembles memory."

As my curiosity about Ruth has led me to return to a text I may not have read since I was a child, I have been surprised to find how many parts of the story resonate with my own, but not in any neat parallel analogical way. These recognitions give me a sense of how a gifted novelist like Mann could enter into the received stories and then recreate them in a way that suggests he knows each character from within. Each scene, each figure, in his recreation becomes vividly alive.

Elimelech isn't like my father, but at a critical moment they made similar decisions. Seeing that connection makes my experience of the biblical story richer and helps me see that moment in my father's life more complexly. I catch glimpses of connections between my mother's story and Naomi's, and somehow I come to feel more compassion for both. I came to the Book of Ruth because of Ruth, but

I find, as I have always found with Greek myths (and with dreams) that I need to pay attention to the associations stirred by each part of the tale (as I found the rabbis did also.)

The biblical story is set in the long ago time before the rise of the monarchy, "in the days when the judges ruled," but without the focus on violence and war found in the Book of Judges. The text is traditionally ascribed to Samuel, the prophet who anointed David king, and is customarily read at Shavuot, the Jewish Pentecost. This festival which honors the giving of the Torah (as the Christian Pentecost celebrated at essentially the same time celebrates the giving of the Holy Spirit) is celebrated on what is said to be King David's birth and death day. Indeed, the Book of Ruth, which relates the story of the courtship of David's great grandparents, can be seen as itself a midrash on the giving of Torah, a midrash that implies that *chesed*, lovingkindness, what one does that cannot be commanded, not law, is the essence of Torah.

Many scholars believe the text was written to be put forward as a subtle but forceful challenge to the laws promulgated by Ezra calling upon Jews (after the return from the exile in Babylon) to divorce their foreign wives. (Though others believe it was probably written during the late monarchy when David's reign was first idealized—and Neusner helps us see how the Christian interpretation of the Book of Ruth as a universalist critique of Jewish particularism turns the book against Judaism.[3])

There are lots of arguments about whether the language is deliberately anachronistic, arguments which entail discussions of the relevance of linguistic usages parallel to those found in presumably late texts like Job, Ezekiel, Second Isaiah, the P parts of the Torah and of the relevance of what seem to be Aramaisms—arguments which lead me to tend to accept the late dating.

I've long known about the changes introduced into Israelite life after the Exile but had not known that the Book of Ruth may have been written in protest against the new emphasis on untainted genealogy. Learning this, returning to the text deliberately open to connections between it and personal experience gave me a new sense of the pain this new law must have inflicted on the husbands and wives affected by it. Among the stories my mother still tells of those first years after Hitler came to power is what it was like for her, after my father had already left for America and we were waiting to join him, to be told (by the magistrate to whom she was required to report every day) that as a good German woman she should divorce her Jewish husband, stay in Germany, and have German babies. That her father, more gently, more lovingly, was giving her the same message cannot have made it easier. (She wouldn't actually have been forced to divorce him, but later on in Germany many gentiles married to Jews had to choose between divorce and the camps.)

The Book of Ruth makes its point against the exclusion of the outsider quite dramatically: it tells us that King David is descended from a Moabite. This, of course, implies that the Messiah (who is to come from the House of David) participates in the same tainted genealogy. Ruth is not just a stranger, a non-Israelite, but a Moabite, from the biblical perspective the most *other* other imaginable. For according to the Torah, although descendants of Esau and even Egyptians may be granted entry into the covenant, Moabites and Ammonites (because they had refused bread and water to the Hebrews during their years of wandering between Egypt and Canaan) are forever to be excluded, and Jews are explicitly forbidden to marry Moabites. A midrash, attempting to reconcile Ruth's story with this prohibition, says that perhaps the Moabite women were blameless. Ruth's bringing Naomi the gleanings from the barley and wheat harvests is a tacit allusion to the ancient tale; she now gives what was once withheld.

When we hear that Ruth is a Moabite we are expected to remember not only this injunction but also the story of how Lot's daughters, believing that they and their father were the only humans left alive after the destruction of Sodom, got Lot drunk and had intercourse with him in the hope of thus preserving the human race. Both daughters got pregnant; one gave birth to Ammon, the other to Moab. There are obvious parallels to Ruth's more innocent, more decorous, lying at the feet of Boaz in the hope of preserving Elimelech's family line.

Yet in another sense Moab does not signify the gentile world but a problem within Israel's own history—and the story of Ruth is a story about the reunion of Lot's and Abraham's family.

The story, however, begins not with Ruth but with Elimelech, a man who had brought his family to Moab from Bethlehem (the House of Bread) at a time of famine (as Jacob's family had once gone to Egypt). The midrashim, of course, link this famine to all the other famines mentioned in the Bible, culminating with the famine not of bread and water but of hearing the words of the Lord in Amos. They seek to figure out which famine this might have been, during the reign of which judge.

Elimelech's wife Naomi (and their two sons) followed him, as Ruth later followed Naomi. Elimelech dies; the two sons marry Moabite women, and their sons die. The place of refuge becomes a place of death. Some midrashim understand these deaths as punishment for Elimelech's leaving his own people at a time of famine and for the sons' marriages to Moabite women (which, some rabbis say, they did without Naomi's permission!). Elimelech is seen as rich and selfish, having the means for such a journey while others don't, fearful of their need (as the Moabites long ago seem to have been fearful that the Hebrews might "lick up all that is around us, as the ox licks up the grass of the field").

I find myself silently protesting this harsh, judgmental view (as, to be fair, do some of the medieval rabbis—who point out Elimelech came just to sojourn, not to live in Moab permanently) and I wonder why. Then I realize: my father left Germany, we left, we were able to leave; my father was warned early and heeded the warning; he had skills that made it possible for him to find a position abroad and eventually the means to enable us to join him. Others stayed, didn't leave or couldn't, were deported, incarcerated, exterminated. Some few made a very different decision from my father's. Leo Baeck, for example, had the opportunity to go to America or Palestine but refused to leave his people. But I can't blame Elimelech or my father for going. I only wish everyone might have gone.

Elimelech disappears from the story early on and Naomi appears as the central figure. Although the book bears Ruth's name and for most readers Ruth is probably the most important person in the story, the story is also Naomi's—she is there from the beginning to the end—and, of course, the story looks different if we focus on her role, try to imagine her perspective, her feelings. (Mann, I know, would have narrated this brilliantly.) Nor is this way of looking at the story foreign to the biblical text. To the chorus of Bethlehem women who greet Naomi upon her return and who give Ruth's child its name as they rejoice, "A son is born to Naomi," Naomi clearly is the more important figure.

Naomi enters the tale as Elimelech's wife, but after his death he becomes just her husband. The story begins in a patriarchal world—Elimelech chooses for his wife and sons, but the men disappear early, belong to the preamble, not to the story.

Left alone, Naomi moves to the center, but as someone (like Demeter) defined by her losses, as someone whom God has forgotten. Her name means "pleasant," but now bitterness is her lot. Bereft of husband and sons, she cannot bear to remain in Moab. When she hears that God has remembered his people in Judah, that the famine in Bethlehem has ended, she decides to return home. When she arrives back in Bethlehem, the women of the town, barely recognizing her, ask, "Can this be Naomi?" (Rashi says they're implying: "See what happened to her because she left?") and she tells them, "Do not call me Naomi. Call me Mara (bitter)."

Naomi seems consumed by her emptiness, her barrenness. She has lost her identity; she is no longer a mother of sons. The theme of infertility looms large in the tale and seems to be all-important to Naomi. Neither Ruth nor the other daughter-in-law, Orpah, have had children. Naomi knows she is too old to bear more sons whom they might marry in accordance with the levirate law—the law which calls upon the brother of a deceased husband to marry his brother's widow so that there might be a son to carry on the dead man's lineage. (Naomi's allusion to levirate marriage prepares for the role Boaz will play later in the tale.)

Because she feels she has nothing left to offer them, Naomi tries, shortly after they have all set out for Judah together, to send Ruth and Orpah back to their *mothers'* houses. This striking locution serves to underline the emphasis on female experience in this singular text. It may also connote that Naomi is sending the two young women back to their own potential motherhood, an interpretation confirmed by her going on to voice a hope that they might yet find new husbands among their own people and bear them children.

The text leaves Naomi's motivation unclear and so the commentators wonder, does Naomi ask them to go back because, as Moabites, they are part of her problem, part of what she wants to leave behind, reminders of her loss, or because of her concern for them? On the one hand, although the narrator speaks of Orpah and Ruth as Naomi's "daughters-in-law," she herself addresses them more tenderly as "daughters" and speaks of them as "sisters" to one another.

On the other, she is silent after Ruth's passionate declaration that she will not let Naomi go on alone. The text says simply "and the two went on," not even that they went on "together," and Naomi utters not a word of relief or gratitude. Naomi's telling the women who come forth to welcome her to Bethlehem that she has come home empty, completely ignoring the presence of Ruth by her side, suggests how totally caught up she is in her own suffering.

And for this suffering she blames God. She feels that though God has remembered his people, as he once remembered Sarah in her barrenness, he has forgotten her. When Naomi speaks of her abandonment by God she, poignantly and pointedly, speaks of him as El Shaddai, the god associated in Genesis with the theme of being fruitful and multiplying, the god who promised Abraham that he would be the father of a multitude. This ancient name for god—a Priestly text in Exodus says it is the name used by the patriarchs before god presented himself as YHVH to Moses—which may have originally meant God of the Mountain or God with Breasts—is typically associated with fertility blessings ("May El Shaddai bless you with the blessings of womb & breast")—just those blessings of which Naomi is deprived. Shaddai, she tells the Bethlehemite women, has made her lot bitter, has brought her back empty, has dealt harshly with her, has brought misfortune upon her. Like Job she seems to be asking, "And why? Of what am I guilty?"

Naomi is not Demeter; her rage and grief exist on a smaller, more human scale. But her tale, too, speaks to us of particularly female experiences of loss—the loss of a husband, of children, of one's own fertility—of the vulnerability of women for whom marriage and children have been self-defining.

In some ways Naomi's story is my mother's. She, too, followed her husband to a foreign land and raised her children there. For a long while her life was full, with children and then with grandchildren, with gardening and poetry, but now in her old age she sees it as empty, barren. She hasn't literally lost her husband or children; they are still alive and very much part of her life, but she has lost the sense that this is enough, that it is meaning-giving, life-giving. She hasn't literally gone back to live in her original homeland, but when she reflects back on what life seemed to promise her when she was young in Germany, what she is aware of is loss. She, too, would say: don't call my life pleasant, call it bitter. And there is no consoling her.

But for me, as for most readers, Ruth is at the center of the story, though not, I've come to see, the figure in it to whom I feel closest. Her name in Hebrew means friendship (though this may be one of those playful etymologies in which both scripture and midrash delight) which may help us see that this is not another story about mother-daughter (or even sister-sister) love but about friendship between women, passionate, committed friendship. I see Ruth as a fiercely *auto-nomos* woman (evident not only when she chooses to go on with Naomi but perhaps even earlier when she chose to marry a foreigner, Naomi's Hebrew son, Mahlon)—a woman who has chosen her own destiny. Yet I am struck that what she chooses is not autonomy and separation but relationship. As Naomi seems to be defined by her losses, Ruth is defined by her choice: henceforward she is the woman who came back with Naomi.

Ruth is said to cling to Naomi, as the Bible calls upon a wife to cling to her husband and asks Israel to cling to God. The Bible also speaks of Jonathan clinging to David, Ruth's great grandson. Jonathan's "soul was knit with the soul of David." David, grieving over Jonathan's death, sang that Jonathan's love to him had been wonderful, "passing the love of women."

At the end of our story the women of Bethlehem, seeing Ruth's love for Naomi, say Ruth is better to Naomi than seven sons. It seems relevant somehow that the Bible's most moving account of a man's love for a man should be thus associated with this tale of a woman's love for a woman. I don't mean that the Book of Ruth is a lesbian story. I don't think it is, but it is a story about love between women, and as a lesbian it is a story that inspires me. (I am always a little amused when Ruth's pledge to Naomi is made part of a heterosexual marriage ceremony without any apparent recognition of the original context in which these words were spoken.)

No doubt our response to Ruth's declaration is inevitably colored by our own experience. I have a friend who reads Ruth's pledge to Naomi and finds herself remembering with horror what it is like to have someone cling to you, make her life dependent on yours, go where you go with no direction of her own. This is her Ruth. It is not mine. To me the love that Ruth expresses in the first words we hear her speak, as well as in her words and actions throughout the rest of the story, is brave and free and generous.

Naomi chooses to return to Bethlehem, and all the connotations of tsuvah, of "return" as signifying a turning back to God, are implicit in her choice. But Ruth is "returning" to a place she's never been. Her "I will go" can be seen in counterpoint to Abraham's silently obedient response to God's call to him to "Go forth." Like Abraham, Ruth is setting out on a journey to an unknown place, but Ruth is not called by anything outside her own heart, and nothing is promised her. She sets forth without family, wealth, or servants. She is choosing Naomi, Naomi's people, Naomi's god.

Many of the traditional commentators, of course, emphasize Ruth's choice of Naomi's god, the Jewish God. There are midrashim that claim that both Ruth and Orpah had converted to Judaism when they married Naomi's sons (even though there was, of course, no conversion ritual in the time of the Judges).

Others imagine an explicit conversion at this point in the tale. Naomi is described as interrupting Ruth's declaration after each phrase to tell her how difficult it is to be a Jew, how it entails keeping the 613 precepts, the strict Sabbath rules, worshipping no other gods, and (striking, in view of what happens later in our story) according to Rashi, a strict prohibition of a man and woman being together alone unless the man is her husband.

But it seems evident to me that Ruth is not so much choosing Naomi's god as choosing Naomi and all that this choice necessarily entails if made without reservation. (And one of the medieval rabbis agrees: "Ruth did all these things because she desired to be with her mother-in-law in whatever circumstances befell her. All this stemmed from the greatness of her love for her.") Phyllis Trible writes: "One female has chosen another female in a world where life depends on men. There is no more radical a decision in all the memories of Israel."[4]

To my mind it is clear—Ruth embraces Naomi's god not out of love of God but out of love of Naomi. Like Marge Piercy (in the poem quoted above) I hear Ruth saying: "I will be a Jew for you." I also believe it is important to note that she is choosing the very god whom Naomi names as the source of her bitterness.

She seems to be saying, your god will be my god no matter what pain and sorrow that commitment may include.

This is clearly why "Ruth" has appeared to me as the name of the shadow self that would have gone with my father to Terezin and Auschwitz. That Ruth is the part of me that would have followed my people to Auschwitz—out of a kind of loyalty to, identification with, a father, a people, not out of a religious commitment to the Hebrew God.

When the two women first find themselves back in Bethlehem, Naomi seems to be still lost in her grief, paralyzed. Ruth is the one to suggest that she go glean after the reapers—because the Israelites had themselves once been sojourners and strangers they were enjoined to leave grains to be gleaned by the needy—and, so the narrator tells us, by luck she begins to do so in the fields of Boaz, Elimelech's well-to-do kinsman. (I think of Keats's description of Ruth "alone, sick for home, amid the alien corn" and am helped to imagine how very alone and yet resilient she is at this point in the story.)

Seeing her, Boaz asks, "Whose maiden is that?" Note the patriarchal assumption—but the answer describes Ruth in terms of her relationship to Naomi, a woman, not to a husband or father. When Boaz learns that the unfamiliar woman in his fields is the Moabite who came back with Naomi, he addresses Ruth as "daughter" and advises her to stay with (cling to) the other women, away from the young male reapers by whom he fears she might be molested. He lets her know that he knows her story, knows she has left father and mother and the land of her birth, knows how good she has been to Naomi.

We may wonder then why all the initiative is left to the women, why Boaz had not himself spontaneously offered to help the two women, and why, once the barley and wheat harvests are over, he feels no concern for their continued well-being. We may also wonder why in the tale Naomi and Boaz never actually meet, why later Naomi couldn't directly raise with him the possibility of his marrying Ruth rather than rely on her rather uncertain scheme, though the biblical text never raises any questions about Boaz's good-heartedness.

Again, I think of a connection to my family history. When my father had gone ahead to America and my mother was left behind with two young children and another on the way and no income beyond the little her parents could spare, almost none of her neighbors or my father's former colleagues seemed to wonder how she was getting by. But twice a week Werner Heisenberg's wife would appear on her bicycle, its basket filled high with eggs and butter, freshly baked bread, and vegetables from her garden.

The text leaves room for much speculation about Boaz. His name implies that he is a man of substance, valor, strength—yet the tale suggests that he may have concerns about aging and sexual potency. It is never clear exactly what his relation to Naomi is—he is a close kinsman but not so close as to have legal responsibility for her welfare. The Bible tells us so very little about him; it does not say whether he was a lifelong bachelor or a recent or longtime widower, whether he'd had children, or just how old he was. Rashi says his first wife died the day Naomi and Ruth returned to Bethlehem. The midrashim generally picture him as old, old enough to be Ruth's father, perhaps to highlight the parallels between the story of Ruth and Boaz and the story of Tamar and Judah.

A story I might as well tell here—for it connects with our story not just as an intended-to-be-noticed parallel but genealogically—since (as we learn later on) Boaz is descended from Tamar and Judah's son, Perez. Judah was Jacob's fourth son, the inheritor of the divine blessing that through Rebecca's trickery had gone to Jacob rather than Esau. Tamar, like Ruth, was a woman who inserted herself into Hebrew history. First married to Judah's eldest son Er, she was, after Er's early death, married in accordance with the levirate law to his second son Onan, who also died young. Fearful for the life of his third son, Judah told Tamar that she must remain a widow until Shelah grew up. But Tamar was determined to be part of Jacob's family (Mann's version of this resolute and deeply thoughtful young woman is unforgettable) and so in disguise as a harlot she inveigled the unsuspecting Judah into having intercourse with her. When Judah learned the truth, and that Tamar was carrying his child (indeed, she turned out to be carrying twins) he acknowledged them as his own. The firstborn was Perez, Boaz's great-great-great-great-grandfather.

Unlike Tamar, Ruth did not herself dream up the plan which leads her to Boaz's threshing floor. Naomi, who by this point in the story seems to have begun moving beyond her grief, suggests to Ruth a plan reminiscent of Rebecca's cunning, reminiscent also of Lot's daughters' seduction of their father and Tamar's of Judah (also a father figure). (A contemporary feminist midrash, acknowledging the riskiness of Naomi's scheme, pictures Naomi praying to God that her plan not put Ruth into a shameful compromising situation.[5]) Gunkel suggests that in the original folktale version of our story there is only a single woman character and that Naomi inveigles Boaz into having intercourse with her when the winnowing is done.

In the scriptural version Naomi directs Ruth to prepare herself by washing, anointing herself, and putting on a special gown—as a bride prepares herself for her wedding bed. And, as Naomi had directed, after Boaz had laid himself down for the night by his grainpile, Ruth stealthily approached and uncovered his feet and lay down beside him. In the middle of the night Boaz awoke, saw her, and asked "Who are you?" (not *whose* this time) as Jacob had asked of the dark stranger with whom he wrestled through the night. And like Jacob, Boaz seems to ask in fear. One wonders if he perceives his unknown nocturnal visitor as a phantom embodiment of his own lust. And though Naomi had said that at this point Boaz would tell Ruth what to do, as the scene unfolds it is actually Ruth who tells him, "Spread your robe"—the word is actually the same as the one used in Ch. 2 for God's protective wings—"over me"—a metaphor for "take in marriage," meant to suggest that Ruth has marriage not just a sexual encounter in mind.

The scene is discreetly reported; it is never said that the two ended up making love. But the feet are often a euphemism for the whole lower body, for the genitals, and "lie beside" is deliberately ambiguous. Boaz praises Ruth for not coming instead to any of the younger men. The midrashim tell us he knows they all desire her. Boaz spreads his robe over Ruth; she lies at his feet until dawn but leaves before anyone might see a woman pass by and recognize her.

Rabbinic midrashim tend to read the Book of Ruth as though it were a love story between Boaz and Ruth and to sexualize their encounter, at the same time denying that it was really sexual. The rabbis praise Boaz for struggling with his own lust and prevailing—"all that night his evil inclination contended with him." They praise Ruth for denying her own desires and choosing an older man able to provide for her and Naomi. Even Naomi (who asks Ruth "Who are you, daughter?" meaning "What happened?" when she returns home in the morning) seems a little worried about what might have happened and what the consequences will be.

Of course, it all works out well. The next day the nearer kinsman of whom Boaz had told Ruth chooses not to act as a redeemer and so Boaz may. (The relation between the laws of redemption—which involves caring for family members in need—and the laws concerning levirate marriage—which concern begetting an heir to carry on a deceased man's lineage—are murky in this tale, never made explicit in the Torah, nor cleared up by the rabbinic midrashim—or in modern scholarly commentaries!)

Many reasons are given for this never-named kinsman's refusal—he was afraid his sons might lose their inheritance were he to have a son with Ruth, he didn't want to have a household containing two women who would always be fighting with one another, he was afraid he would die as Mahlon and Chilion had, he didn't know Moabite women were excluded from the injunction against

Moabites. (One midrashim says that Boaz announced this new law about the women during the threshing floor scene.)

Boaz's marriage vows are surely not couched in the language of romantic love: "I am acquiring from Naomi all that belonged to Elimelech and all that belonged to Chilion and Mahlon. I am also acquiring Ruth the Moabite, the wife of Mahlon, as my wife so…that the name of the deceased may not disappear from among his kinsmen."

Boaz was not obligated by the laws of levirate marriage to marry Ruth; his agreeing to do so was a kind of metaphorical extension of those laws, a *chesed* version of a *mitzvot*.

Unlike some other contemporary readers of the story, I do not see this marriage as simply an ugly example of "the traffic in women," as just another version of the old story of a young woman giving herself to an old man for food.[6] I note that in sending Ruth to Boaz, Naomi says she is hoping to help her find a home where she may be happy and that Boaz seems to be marrying Ruth not out of avarice or lust but because of his respect for her loyalty to Naomi. It is as though he loves her for her love of Naomi (as Ruth loved Naomi's God out of her love for Naomi).

The elders of the community add their blessing after Boaz has spoken, by asking God to make the woman coming into his house "like Leah and Rachel." This leads me to remember that, as far as I know, the only two women, other than Naomi and Ruth, whose conversation with one another is directly presented in a biblical text are Rachel and Leah. Among the most unforgettable passages in *Joseph and His Brothers* are those in which Mann presents the ambivalent and always competitive love for one another between these two sisters who shared a household lifelong—and a husband. Obviously there is a barely hidden sense in which Naomi and Ruth share a husband too: when Ruth gives birth to Boaz's son, the chorus of Bethlehem women announce that a son has been born to Naomi!

The elders' blessing was surely consciously meant only as an expression of their hope that the marriage of Boaz and Ruth would be a fruitful one. And, indeed, God "gives Ruth conception"—one rabbi says that he means he gave her an ovary which she must have been missing given her long previous barrenness. Ruth gives birth to a son Obed who becomes the progenitor of the House of David, as the children of Rachel and Leah became the forefathers of the twelve tribes of Israel.

After the marriage and the conception of this child, Boaz disappears from the story. As though to highlight the notion that Boaz enters the story only so that

Ruth the Moabite and Boaz's determined ancestress Tamar might both be brought into the lineage that issues in David (and eventually in the Messiah) a midrashic tradition claims that Obed was conceived on the night of the wedding, which was also, we are told, the last night of Boaz's life.

As I read the story, Ruth marries Boaz so that the two women can stay together; the marriage is pragmatic not romantic, yet based on love, the women's love for one another. (The only time the word "love" appears in the story is when the townswomen praise Ruth's love for Naomi as better than having seven sons.) When Ruth gives birth to her child she seems happy to give him to Naomi to hold, to have Naomi become his foster mother, to allow the neighbor women to give him his name. It is as though having a son was never as important to her as she knew it was to Naomi. It is almost as if, with the birth of Obed, Naomi is given a second family, as Job is in the epilogue to his story. In a sense Ruth may be serving as a surrogate mother for Naomi, as Hagar did for Sarah, as Leah's and Rachel's handmaidens did for them, but the story suggests she chooses to do so out of love, knowing (as Naomi's women friends also knew) that the child would renew Naomi's life and sustain her old age. I imagine the relationship between Naomi and Ruth as enriched by their sharing of Ruth's child, as I know my relationship with my mother was deepened and expanded when I brought my children to her and let her care for them.

Ruth's handing her son over to Naomi is but another expression of that same *chesed* that leads her to follow Naomi to Bethlehem. I find her extraordinary. And, although my closer study of her and her story only confirms my hunch that "Ruth" is the right name for that shadow self who would have ended up in an extermination camp, I do not imagine that I—whatever life I might have led, the one I've actually led here in America, the one I might have led as a German gentile girl exposed to all the pressures of my contemporaries' surrounding enthusiasm for Hitler, or the one I might have led in Hitler's camps—would ever have been so extraordinary, so bravely risk-taking, so loyal, so determined.

And so I have come to recognize that the figure in the tale with whom I actually most identify is Orpah, the other Moabite daughter-in-law. Initially Orpah too protests that she will return with Naomi, but as Naomi again asks the two young women to turn back and return to their mothers' houses, Orpah weeps and kisses Naomi good-bye. I agree with Cynthia Ozick that Orpah is never, never to be blamed for staying home, for making the more conventional, the ordinary choice.[7] She belongs to the story as much as Ruth, as Ruth's necessary foil, as Ismene (whom George Steiner called "the most beauteous measure of the ordinary"[8]) belongs in the story of Antigone. I have come to honor these women who choose the ordinary rather than the extraordinary, who choose survival. The life I've actually lived is more Orpah's than Ruth's, a safe and in many ways conventional life. I am aware of having consciously chosen such a life. I can even remember the moment of choosing. Shortly after the end of the Second World War when I had just graduated from college and was pregnant with my first child, I went back to Germany for the first time since I'd left when I was four. There I met a young German man, just a few years older than I, who had survived the camps. I remember asking him what, in the light of all that had happened, I should do with my life. "Live in a way that shows it is still possible to live an ordinary mostly happy human life," he told me. And so I have tried to do.

What Orpah loses is the three thousand years of being part of the Jewish story, which is what I, in the life I've actually lived, have also been deprived of. And yet, in a sense, both of us *are* part of the story.

As I hope has been clear to you—my reading of the Book of Ruth is not put forward as an authoritative interpretation. That was never the aim. I have tried simply to suggest how rich this tale is, how full of complications and how moving, how it has pulled me to learn more about it and the traditions surrounding it than I had any need to do beyond pure fascination—and to try to share with you how first this part of the story and then that illuminate my own experience—and how in turn my own experience has led to me to understand the text in a particular way.

Notes

1. See Judith A. Katz and Gail Twersky Reimer, eds., *Reading Ruth: Contemporary Women Reclaim a Sacred Story* (Ballantine, 1994). My own rereading has been very influenced by the many fine essays in this book.

2. Marge Piercy, "The Book of Ruth and Naomi," *Mars and Her Children* (Knopf, 1992) included in Katz and Reimer, 159.

3. Jacob Neusner, *The Mother of the Messiah in Judaism: The Book of Ruth* (Valley Forge: Trinity Press, 1993) 5.

4. Phyllis Trible, "A Human Comedy," *God and the Rhetoric of Sexuality* (Fortress Press) 173.

5. Ruth H. Sohn, "Verse by Verse," in Katz and Reimer, 24.

6. See for example Norma Rosen, "Dialogue on Devotion," in Katz and Reimer, 350.

7. Cynthia Ozick, "Ruth," *Metaphors and Memory* (Knopf, 1989), included in Katz and Reimer, 224.

8. George Steiner, *Antigones* (Oxford University Press, 1984) 121.

3

The Biblical Book of Genesis:
Beginnings, Endings,
and New Beginnings

I seem always to be more shaped by the Zeitgeist than I consciously realize. I remember, for example, how when I was in my 20s my husband's and my decision that we wanted to have four or five children seemed so entirely our own, one that grew out of our having each been the oldest of three in our families of origin. Yet now, looking back, I can see how in the early 1950s, shortly after the end of the Second World War, everyone was having large families, that it wasn't after all an entirely individual choice. I also remember how in my first year here in San Diego I had a dream which led me to "Go in search of Her," to become deeply involved with trying to understand the relevance of Greek goddess traditions to my own self-understanding (and, by extension, to that of other contemporary women and perhaps even some men)—and then how I soon discovered that at almost the same moment elsewhere in the country many other women—I am thinking particularly of Merlin Stone, Charlene Spretnak, Starhawk, and Carol Christ—were engaged in much the same exploration.

Well, it has happened again!

For the last two years I have teaching at Pacifica Graduate Institute in a new Ph.D. program in Mythological Studies and last year I agreed that this spring I would teach a course on the Mythologies of the Monotheisms. So this fall as I was preparing my syllabus, knowing that I would, of course, begin with the stories in Genesis, I saw an advertisement for a Bill Moyers PBS series to be devoted to the biblical book of Genesis. A few weeks later at the annual meeting of the American Academy of Religion as I wandered up and down the aisles of the book display rooms, I found book after book devoted to Genesis: three new translations and almost a dozen commentaries or interpretations. Which led me to realize that once again there was something going on in the culture at large: Genesis is "in," it's hot, it's new. It even made the cover of *Time* and an article in the "Week in Review" section of the *New York Times*.

So of course I'm interested in *WHY*? Why this burgeoning of interest in the first book of the Hebrew Bible? It doesn't seem to be a sign of increased piety or part of the revival of fundamentalism. Indeed, my hope is that it might even be a sign that the religious right's stranglehold on the Bible is finally being challenged, that the interest grows out of a recognition that these stories belong to all of us—Jews and Christians and Muslims, believers and unbelievers, men and women, even feminist women like myself, even those among us whose religious heritage has no connection with the biblical tradition but who live in this culture which has been so profoundly shaped by it.

Moyers says that because he created his program for the sake of a collective healing, he sought to bring together representatives of all these different perspectives, to include not only biblical scholars and preachers but also literature professors and writers and therapists. He looked for participants able to be forthrightly honest about their own views and respectful of other radically differing views. He hoped that talking together about these stories first told millennia ago might open the way for a different kind of religious discourse. Partly because they are wonderful stories, stories that seem to invite retelling, reflection, remembering and reimagining—and because they are the foundational stories of western culture. As, of course, Greek myths also are—although traditionally, because of their association with a still dominant religious culture, we have often felt reluctant to look at the biblical stories as freely as we do the Greek ones.

But the question is still: *WHY NOW*? Why now this evidently widespread interest in looking anew at these stories that have been there all along? I believe it may have something (not by any means everything) to do with the approach of the millennium, with the hopes and anxieties and just plain wonder associated with the approach of 2000 and 2001. Of course, for many of us this is just an arbitrary date, based on an ancient miscalculation about the most likely date of Jesus of Nazareth's birth. Yet I suspect that this may not be wholly true for even the most skeptical among us. I vividly remember as a small child wondering if I would still be alive in 2000. My father was born in 1901, at the very beginning of the twentieth century; so the thought that I might be around at its end seemed somehow magical. The year 2000 seemed to signify some kind of big completion, a turning point, an ending and a new beginning. Neither then nor now was there any particular content to this anticipation—just the mystery of endings and of beginnings. An ending and a beginning of a different magnitude than more personal events like a marriage or the birth of a child or grandchild, because more communal, more cosmic, more archetypal.

It seems always to be true that a heightened sense of the approach of an ending awakens interest in stories of origin, and it makes a lot of sense that the strange mixture of fear and fascination associated with the apocalyptic imagination should encourage a renewed involvement with *these* stories of origin. For the stories of Genesis are the stories that lie at the foundation of the tradition that issues in western apocalyptic speculation. These are our culture's stories about how it began, about the beginning of the world but more particularly about the beginnings of human history—and like all stories of origin they are meant to show how things came to be as they *are* (and will be).

The popularity of Moyers' television series and of the spate of new books suggest a view of the Genesis stories as being not too holy to question—or too irrelevant to take seriously. In a sense this has always been more true of the Jewish midrashic tradition than of the Christian exegetical one. Midrash entails close readings of the biblical texts, noting the contradictions and tensions, filling in the gaps and ambiguities. The rabbis believed that such intense and imaginative questioning is what keeps the Bible alive; scripture is seen as inviting these expansions.

Perhaps now many of us are ready to look at this literature critically and imaginatively, to look at these stories *as stories,* as, if you will (and I do) as *myths.*

As I mentioned last year, at the very beginning of my teaching career at Rutgers (almost 35 years ago now) I taught Hebrew Scriptures, but never did so during my almost twenty years here at SDSU. So turning to this literature again now is a new beginning for me and I have become very aware how different it is to look at it through a mythological studies lens rather than through a religious studies lens. In this context it's not a question of talking about some mythic elements—borrowed and reworked or foreign and extraneous—that pop up here and there in the Bible but about looking at the whole Bible as a myth system. Not only the stories about the creation of the world, about the flood or the tower of Babel, but also those about David and Solomon. Not only Lilith but also Eve. Not only the golden calf but also the stone tablets engraved with the ten commandments.

Of course, it is often maintained that polytheistic traditions are mythmaking, whereas monotheistic traditions are mythless. The two most often consulted overviews of world mythology, the *New Larousse Encyclopedia of Mythology* and the two-volume *Mythologies* edited by Yves Bonnefoy, for example, do not include Jewish, Christian, or Muslim tradition. This view is put forward both by adherents of monotheism: monotheism is free of myth; a big gain—and by its detractors: myth is missing from monotheism; a big loss.

But way back when I wrote my doctoral dissertation on the Jewish philosopher Martin Buber, I learned from him that myth is "the nurturing soul of all religion," and that mythology and monotheism are not mutually exclusive.[1] Buber warns against making our definition of myth too narrow. He views myth as including all accounts of "physically real events understood as divine events," not just tales about physically present divine beings. Because Jewish monotheism views all things and events as utterances of God, because for it an event was only worth telling when grasped in its divine significance, the Jews of antiquity, he says, could tell a story only mythically.

So, there's myth in the Hebrew Bible, albeit a different form of myth. The relation to humankind is central to this God, not incidental as it is in most mythologies. He wouldn't be who he is apart from this relation. For these stories are not just accounts of God's activities and how they affect humans; they also recount how humans influence God. There is real dialogue, real conversation between this God and his human creatures. The world is God's word—but he seeks response and is changed by that response. (Think for instance of how Moses persuades a very reluctant YHVH to make a second set of the tablets inscribed with the ten commandments or how Abraham bargains him down when he is threatening Sodom and Gomorrah.)

Buber speaks of Biblical myth as the myth of the caller and the called, of the I and the You. He notes the repetitive pattern: God's always unexpected, unsought, unwelcome, imperious "YOU," and the human response "Here I am" (and also "Please not me; Please find someone else.") The notion that Hebraic myth is a different kind of myth is, of course, an integral part of the biblical myth. The Bible itself presents the origin of monotheism as a mystery, as a sudden event, not a gradual unfolding. Monotheism arises in response to an unanticipated revelation, not in response to persistent religious seeking. It comes with one of those *YOU*'s. The out of the blue "you" to Abraham: "Go from your country and your kindred and your father's house to the land that I will show you." Leave everything you've known behind, all on the basis of a promise about a land I that I say I will someday get around to showing you. The equally unprepared-for "you" addressed to Moses: "I will send you to Pharaoh that you may bring forth my people." When Moses asks, "Why me?" he is given the on the surface non sequitur answer, "I shall be with you."

Obviously this is the view *within the myth*. Modern historians would tell the story quite differently. They would talk about the slow emergence of Hebraic monotheism, would say that the Bible's view of a clear-cut distinction between Canaanite and Hebraic religion preceding the fall of the Northern Kingdom represents a retrospective denial of Israel's own past. Indeed, they would insist that before the exile radical monotheism was essentially the fantasy of a few prophets, not shared by the people, the priests or the kings.[2] Even in the Decalogue what is commanded is monolatry—"Have no other gods before me," not "There are no other gods." The covenant presupposes a polytheistic context.

Thus, to understand the biblical perspective seems to require recognizing both that the Bible takes history more seriously than any other mythology *and* that it doesn't present history literally. The emphasis falls on encounters between God and humans, on events that happen in our world, in history. Yet, as Northrop Frye notes, there is in the Bible "an exuberant repudiation of everything we are accustomed to think of as historical evidence."[3] To look at history as the arena of God's revelation is to adopt a *mythic* view of history.

What the Bible does offer is not objective history but an emphasis on linear (rather than cyclical) time as the kind of time that really matters. The notion of time as having what Heidegger called "three ecstasies"—past, present, and future—which is so fundamental to our western sensibilities, has its origins here. The past is over, done with, irretrievable. The present is a time of decision, choice, response-ability. The future is genuinely open, the realm of possibility. Time moves forward from a discrete beginning point, through an interim period (the period in which Abraham and Moses and *we* live) towards a goal, a culmination. What happens in the interim period is crucial; how we respond to the events and persons we encounter will determine whether and when that goal is reached. It's not much of a stretch to see how this issues in a focus on unique never-before moments and in a view of the human self that gives precedence to the will and to individuality.

Not God alone but we-with-God determine what will happen in the future.[4] For, as I've already noted, the Biblical God is a God for whom the relation to humankind is pivotal. Jack Miles in his *God: A Biography*[5] relates this to the inescapable and profound loneliness of this *only* God who has no parents, no siblings, no spouse. As Miles puts it, "The Bible opens with God talking to himself," and creating us to assuage his loneliness. Miles suggests that the unique interdependence between this god and humans issues in their endlessly complaining about each other; he connects the extravagant anger this god sometimes directs at humans as being a consequence of wanting too much from them. Miles also proposes that this god creates humans out of a longing to know himself; he creates us in his image so he'll have a self-image. (This reminds me of one of my favorite passages in Thomas Mann's *Joseph and His Brothers*, the section called "How Abraham Found God," which speaks of "the extraordinary involutions" of their relationship, so that in a sense each creates the other.)

Miles writes about the Biblical God as a literary figure. I guess I'd prefer to speak of him as (like all gods) a mythical figure, which means saying that Yahweh IS the stories told about him. The myths about him define the community. We are the people who tell these stories.

This raises the question of the "we"—always such a slippery word to introduce into a talk or a paper. Originally these stories served (as Frye says a myth system always does) "to draw a circumference around a human community," the Hebrews of ancient Israel.[6] So I was using the "we" rhetorically to refer to "them." Yet I do believe this "we" does also include "us." For I believe it is important to recognize the degree to which all of us, religious or secular, men or women, in our culture are shaped by this view of God, this view of the relation between God and humankind.

Probably I don't need to say that I am fully aware of some of the costs of this particular mythology, which envisions the divine almost solely in male terms, gives humans dominion over the earth, and condones the conquest of indigenous peoples. Though often angry and sometimes vindictive, this God is nevertheless said to be so unequivocally good that all evil and suffering are ascribed to human sin and failure. The way these views have supported ecological devastation, misogyny, racism, and a culture of guilt are to my mind obvious. Yet I believe that when acknowledging these costs we must also acknowledge the gifts we owe to this mythology: the dream of social justice (so that the Bible itself has been the primary source of the critique which discerns and contests its shortcomings), science (which is unimaginable apart from the Bible's view of nature as at our disposal), the valorization of the individual ego (which I believe is deeply ingrained in all westerners no matter how drawn they be to eastern philosophies). It doesn't take much thought to recognize that there is no way of wholly divorcing the costs from the gifts.

So you can see why I think it so important for us to know the stories that shape *us*—not just our culture but us, consciously and unconsciously. The recent interest in Genesis that I spoke of at the beginning of this talk confirms the power that these stories still hold. As I looked at the Moyers television series I was especially struck by how the participants in their discussions of the ancient stories kept bringing in stories from their own lives—their divorces, their struggles with fathers, their concerns about their children or about their work. They were, Moyers noted, talking about the stories not as yesterday's news but as today's. I enjoyed this and was sometimes deeply moved, but I also found myself wondering: does this to some degree strip the tales of awe and aura? Do the stories get reduced to our own size? Does it make them too contemporary? Does this focus on the relevance of these stories to our daily lives pose the danger of leaching them of their mythic archetypal power?

It's a subtle issue; of course, we need to feel there is a connection between the Biblical stories and our stories. This not only gives us a way into the stories, it also helps us gain access to archetypal aspects of our experience. Yet I do believe there is some danger of losing a sense of the way these stories are somehow bigger, more numinous, full of meanings we can't immediately grasp; that they have the power to challenge our way of looking at things not just confirm it. I also believe that when we focus on the personal relevance of individual stories we may tend to lose sight of ways these stories are *linked*, the way they get their power from recurring and developing themes. (This is, of course, a danger also posed by an emphasis on "Source Theory"—for so long the dominant trend in Christian biblical scholarship—and its focus on taking the given text apart and trying to learn as much as one can about the constituent parts that were eventually woven into the text as we now have it.)

Talking a little about some of the translations of Genesis may help me clarify what I'm trying to say. The various group translations—the Revised Standard Version, the English Bible, the Jerusalem Bible, the Jewish Publication Society's *Tanakh*—all try to make the Bible's perspective more available, to render it in 20th-century idiomatic language and thus make its meaning as clear as possible. "In pursuit of clarity the pungent and concrete is often made abstract and bland."[7]

Between 1925 and 1961 Buber (along with Franz Rosenzweig) tried to create a very different kind of translation of the Hebrew Bible into German, and two years ago Emmet Fox published *The Five Books Of Moses* in which he sought to do in English the same kind of thing Buber and Rosenzweig had tried to do in German. These translations aim to communicate how truly alien the Biblical world and its language is. They seek to make us work to try to understand it, to force attentive reading. They look for ways of reproducing the rhythms and syntax of the original Hebrew, to show how much it relies on repetition and on word play. They carefully always use the same German or English word for the same Hebrew one. They deliberately try to make the ambiguities in the text visible, rather than to eliminate them or explain them. They want to give us a sense of the concreteness of the Biblical imagination. (The example that comes to mind is that where other translations write of an "altar," these translations give us the more literally exact "slaughter table.") They invite us to read the Bible as though we had never encountered it before.

Very different is the *Genesis* that the poet Stephen Mitchell published just this year. Mitchell is my favorite translator of Rainer Maria Rilke and I value his versions of the *Tao Te Ching* and of the Book of Job, but I must say I was disappointed in this most recent project. Mitchell relies heavily on Source Theory and speaks of the redactors' (the post-exilic editors who gave the Torah its final form) disservice to the original authors. He says he's offended and bored by what are commonly called the "P" (for the so-called "Priestly" post-exilic source) passages, particularly the genealogies, so he decides to just omit them! He makes no effort to distinguish prose passages in the original from poetic, and cavalierly eliminates repetitions that he sees as redundant.

Robert Alter, by contrast, in his *Genesis: Translation and Commentary,* emphasizes the genius of the redactors (and thus reminds me that Buber once said that he understood the "R," the shorthand symbol which Biblical scholars often use to refer to the post-exilic redactors of the Torah, as meaning "Rabbenau," our teacher.) Alter writes of how the redactor (he tends to use the singular) weaves together tellings from many different periods and perspectives and succeeds in creating a whole, a focused coherent narrative, which honors the parts out of which it is composed. He notes how this gifted editor by beginning with the late "P" account of the creation of the universe sets the whole within a cosmic frame. He notes how the "P" genealogies (of which Mitchell is so dismissive) are inserted to mark really significant transitions. Alter also notes that the phrase usually translated as "these are the generations" could as appropriately be rendered as "these are the *stories*." He helps us see how much implicit commentary is conveyed simply by the ordering of stories. For instance, how the account of the banishment of Ishmael, Abraham's first son, is immediately followed by the story of Abraham's being commanded to sacrifice his other son, Isaac. And how this in turn is immediately followed by the announcement of Sarah's death, as though (the rabbis suggested this long ago) she had died of heartbreak over what Abraham had been willing to do without even a word to her. Alter calls our attention to significant repetitions, to how the "Go Forth" to Abraham in Genesis 12, where Abraham is called upon to leave the past behind is echoed in the "Go Forth" of Genesis 22, where he is called upon to sacrifice the son who symbolizes the promised future.

There are so many wonderful stories in Genesis, stories I obviously don't even have the time to name here, much less to tell. I'd urge you to rent the Moyers tapes, to read Alter's translation with its illuminating commentary, or Peter Pitzele's fine *Our Father's Wells,* or Alicia Oistriker's *The Nakedness of the Fathers.*

But there is a particular recurring theme I want to highlight as central to my own understanding of this book: the theme of rivalry between brothers. I could, of course, have chosen to speak of the women in Genesis—and there are some wonderful stories about women, about Eve, about Sarah and Hagar, and Rebecca, and Rachel and Leah and Dinah, and Tamar. I choose instead to turn to the brother theme because of the way it relates to my theme of Beginnings and Endings and New Beginnings.

The theme of brother rivalry is there from the very beginning, in the story about the first fully human beings, the first born-in-history figures, Cain and Abel. As Alicia Oistriker writes: "To make a long story short, awful as it is, at some (early) point we have to have the first murder. We have to…[God] doesn't know exactly why he wanted to choose between the two, preferring one, He only knows that he had to."[8] But then over and over, the same story, or almost the same story. Noah's sons. Ishmael and Isaac, though we are told that they do come back together to bury Abraham. Jacob and Esau, already struggling with one another in the womb. Jacob's stealing of the birthright and the blessing due his older brother, his flight and the long years away from home during which he learns that even tricksters get tricked. The beautiful reconciliation scene between these two brothers the morning after Jacob's night of wrestling with the stranger (who may be the wronged brother or his own guilt or God—or, more likely, all of the above). Jacob is deeply moved by Esau's open-hearted forgiveness and yet still wary. He refuses Esau's invitation to come settle near by and instead moves far away enough to foil any further rivalry.

And then there is Joseph, Joseph and his brothers. This is a story I imagine you all remember. The narcissism of the son who knows full well that he's his father's favorite. The murderous resentment of his older brothers. Their not quite daring to kill him after all, but nonetheless letting Jacob believe that his son has been killed. Joseph's rescue from the well. All the years in Egypt with their ups and downs and new ups. But I want to focus on the very last scene in Genesis. It takes place after the family has been reunited in Egypt, and after Jacob's death. With their father gone, Joseph's older brothers are fearful that Joseph might now show that he's not really wholly forgiven them after all:

When Joseph's brothers saw that their father was dead, they said, "What if Joseph still bears a grudge against us and pays us back for all the wrong we did him!" So they sent this message to Joseph, "Before his death your father left this instruction: So shall you say to Joseph, 'Forgive, I urge you, the offense and guilt of your brothers who treated you so harshly.' Therefore, please forgive the offense of the servants of the God of your father." And Joseph was in tears as they spoke to him.[9]

I find Thomas Mann's version of Joseph's reply even more beautiful than the beautiful words of the Biblical text, so I am going to use it:

> When you talk to me about forgiveness, it seems to me you have missed the meaning of the whole story we are in. I do not blame you for that. One can easily be in a story and not understand it. Perhaps that is the way it ought to be and I am to blame myself for always knowing far too well what was being played. Did you not hear from the father's own lips, when he gave me my blessing, that my life has always been only a play and a pattern? Did he remember, when he pronounced judgment on you, the bad things which happened between you and me? No, he kept quiet about them, because he too was in the play, God's play. I was protected by him when I had to rub you all the wrong way and provoke you to evil in my crude childishness that cried to heaven. God turned it all to good, for I came to feed many people and so I was forced to mature a bit. But if it is a question of pardon between us human beings, then it is I myself must beg for it, for you had perforce to be cast in the villain's part so that things might turn out as they did. So now am I to use the might of Pharaoh simply because I command it, to avenge myself for three days' discipline in the well and so make ill again what God has made good? I could laugh at the thought....
>
> Thus he spoke to them and they laughed and wept together and stretched out their hands as he stood among them and touched him, and he too caressed them with his hands. And so endeth the beautiful story and God-invention of *JOSEPH AND HIS BROTHERS*.[10]

I find this a beautiful ending, a moving ending, to a book full of many painful moments—this recognition that there are moments of reconciliation, of forgiveness, of harmony, of peace. Of course, the story doesn't really end there. There will be many later moments of tension, of conflict, and of suffering. But the despair-bringing moments are never the whole story. There are endings—and there are new beginnings.

Notes

1. Martin Buber, "Myth in Judaism," *On Judaism* (New York: Schocken, 1972) 95–107.

2. Cf. Mark S. Smith, *The Early History of God: Yahweh and the Other Deities in Ancient Israel* (New York: Harper & Row, 1990) and Israel Finkelstein and Neil Asher Silberman, *The Bible Unearthed* (New York: Free Press, 2001).

3. Northrop Frye, *The Great Code: The Bible and Literature* (San Diego: Harcourt Brace Jovanovich, 1982) 42.

4. This is, of course, not true of the apocalyptic perspective that gains momentum in the post-exilic period when confidence that we humans might ever learn to live together in a peaceful and just way has for many eroded, so that the only hope is that God will create the longed for blissful world for us, for the deserving among us.

5. Jack Miles, *God: A Biography* (New York: Vintage, 1995).

6. Frye, 37.

7. Robert Alter, *Genesis: Translation and Commentary* (New York: Norton, 1996) xii.

8. Alicia Oistriker, *The Nakedness of the Fathers: Biblical Visions and Revisions* (New Brunswick: Rutgers University Press, 1994) 35.

9. *Tanakh: A New Translation of the Holy Scriptures According to the Traditional Hebrew Text* (Philadelphia: The Jewish Publication Society, 1985) 83.

10. Thomas Mann, *Joseph and His Brothers* (New York: Knopf, 1983) 1207.

4

It's Not So Simple After All: Auschwitz, the Death of God, the Rebirth of the Goddess

My lecture this year will explore some ideas that are still new, still in process, not yet fully worked out, but that nonetheless feel important to me—and that are, I recognize, are in some ways a continuation of themes explored in these lectures in earlier years.

The first idea is fairly simple and in retrospect almost embarrassingly obvious—though even it represents a recognition relatively new to me. I can see now that the problems that the Holocaust poses for the biblical understanding of God as the all powerful and wholly just Lord of History helped prepare the way for a renewal of interest in ancient goddess traditions. That is, Auschwitz prepared the way for the "Death of God" and the "Death of God" in turn helped prepare the way for the "Rebirth of the Goddess."

The second, the idea that's not so simple after all, may be more problematic, less obvious and perhaps less persuasive, and is almost surely a more idiosyncratic, more personal conclusion. Continued reflection on the Holocaust has led me to believe that the understanding of evil I find in goddess traditions isn't fully adequate either and that, somewhat to my own surprise, I have recently found myself returning to some aspects of the biblical view of things!

So my talk has four parts: Beginning with Auschwitz, the Death of the Biblical God, The Rebirth of the Goddess, A ReVisioning of the Biblical Understanding of Evil.

Beginning With Auschwitz

I first started thinking along these lines last fall as I was preparing to be part of a panel at a session of the annual meeting of the American Academy of Religion devoted to Carol Christ's two most recent books, *Odyssey With The Goddess* and *Rebirth Of The Goddess*. I noted then how both Carol and I, well before we had become involved with the goddesses, had begun our work as theologians under the shadow of the Holocaust. In the mid 1960s I had written my doctoral dissertation on Martin Buber with a focus on his understanding of the eclipse of God in the contemporary world. A few years later Carol wrote hers on Elie Wiesel and his experience as an adolescent at Auschwitz of being abandoned by God, his experience of God's silence and absence. Almost a decade intervened before we published our first essays about the role that goddesses might play in the religious experience of contemporary women: her now classic article, "Why Women Need the Goddess;" and "Persephone in Hades," which became the starting-point for my book, *The Goddess.*

As I reflected on this trajectory I began to wonder if there might not be more continuity than either of us had consciously realized. Certainly, as my previous lectures in this series indicate, I have felt compelled in recent years to return to the role the Holocaust has played in my own life. I have come to recognize that in some ways the Holocaust (or, as I'd prefer to say, the Shoah—for I feel deeply how radically the word Holocaust, with its connotations of a willing sacrifice, misrepresents the wanton murder perpetrated by the Nazis) is for me an inescapable starting-point. I know that this is to some degree the consequence of my personal history. As you may recall, I was born in Germany in 1931. My father's father was Jewish. My father was a university professor who lost his position almost as soon as Hitler came to power in 1933. By 1935 my parents, my two siblings, and I were safely settled in New Jersey.

So in outward practical ways we suffered very little. Yet I agree with Richard Rubenstein that "for those of us who lived through the terrible years, whether in safety or as victims, the Shoah conditions the way we encounter all things sacred and profane."[1] Because for me the Shoah epitomizes the evil we humans are capable of doing against one another, I know that my understanding of our human being-here must include recognition of this capacity, must come to terms with what Auschwitz reveals about the cruelty and vulnerability of our human being-here. This does not mean I see evil as only evident, as only real or important, when it takes on the dimensions of what happened in the Nazi extermination camps, but simply that looking at the horrors perpetrated by what seem to have mostly been rather ordinary human beings—not beasts, not demons—can make us see some things that seem to be true of human beings as such, including ourselves.

That is, Auschwitz reveals not the inhumanity of humankind, but our humanity in its most terrifying aspect—and it seems terribly important to me that we take this aspect seriously. I believe we miss the fullness of what we might learn from the Shoah if it leads us to too easy, too complacent an identification with the victims. If it does not also leads us to ask about our relation to the perpetrators and to the bystanders. If we do not recognize the perpetrators as being overtaken by resentments, temptations, fears which we can recognize in ourselves. Even though, of course, we would also want to hope that we would not be wholly overtaken by these feelings, would not fall into what Martin Buber calls "radical evil."

By this phrase Buber meant to point to a persisting in evil, a coming to gloat in doing evil, which entails a denial of any limits, a refusal to recognize ourselves as standing in relation to any Beyond, any standard outside ourselves, any sense of a good to which we are answerable. Buber sees Auschwitz, sees radical evil, as expressing a vehement denial of the biblical God who demands we be moral, a vehement denial of what he calls the Eternal Thou—but also a vehement denial of the thou-ness of the actual human persons we encounter, a vehement denial of our being essentially in relation to human others. We need to remember that the Nazis didn't just kill the Jews, but saw them as vermin rather than as fellow humans. So that for them participating in genocide was compatible with being good husbands and fathers. Indeed, they sought to so humiliate and degrade their victims as to make these victims lose *their* trust in others, their sense of their own personhood.

The Death Of God

The Shoah taught me to see the problem of evil as a human problem, an anthropological problem, rather than as a theological one. It seems evident to me that not God but we humans were responsible for the Shoah. I have come to believe that wrestling with the problems the Shoah poses for traditional Jewish and Christian theology, for the belief that history is the arena of God's revelation and the correlative belief that therefore God must have in some way permitted, even intended, the horrors of Auschwitz (and thus, most perniciously, that the gas chambers were in some mysterious way a deserved punishment) is a large part of what led me (and some of my closest feminist theologian friends, women such as Carol Christ and Naomi Goldenberg) to turn from the biblical god to the goddess or (at least in my case) to the goddesses.

As it also led Richard Rubenstein (actually earlier than it led us)—as he wrote in his 1966 book *After Auschwitz*—to turn from the God of history to the long disregarded divinities of earth, the ancient Canaanite divinities, Baal and Anath and Astarte. Rubenstein spoke of the death of the biblical God, not with the celebratory voice of some of the Christian "Death of God" theologians, but rather out of a somber conviction that he could no longer accept an ideology which equated human suffering with divine retribution nor one which saw God only as love:

> We have been cast up absurdly and without reason into a world which knows no warmth, concern, care, fellowship, or love save that which we bestow upon one another....
>
> We have turned away from the God of history to share the tragic fatalities of the God of nature.... After the death camps, life in and of itself, lived and enjoyed in its own terms, without any superordinate values or special theological relationships, becomes important for Jews.... Life need not have any meta-historical meanings to be worthwhile.... This need for sanity within the community has been underscored by our rediscovery of Israel's earth and the lost divinities of that earth. Once again we have come in contact with those powers of life and death which engendered men's feelings about Baal, Astarte, and Anath. These powers have again become decisive in our religious life.[2]

Auschwitz radically reopens the age-old problem of theodicy, the problem of how to reconcile the notion of the goodness and power of god with what actually happens. As Archibald MacLeish put it in his poetic drama *J.B.*:

> If god is good he is not god,
> If god is god he is not good.
> Take the even, take the odd,
> I would not stay here if I could,
> Except for the little green leaves in the wood
> And the wind out on the water.[3]

I have come to believe that at least some of us feminists turned away from the biblical God not only because he was a male god and we hungered for images of the divine which would also honor the sacrality of female power and of the female body—but also because of our questioning of a vision of the divine which condones the conquest of indigenous peoples, which gives humans unrestrained dominion over the earth, which sees the divine as all good and all powerful and so makes all suffering, all that goes wrong, the consequence of human sin. We had become painfully aware of the costs of this vision of the divine in relation to the oppression of women (and as we eventually realized to the oppression of men, as well) and to the exploitation of the natural world.

We must also have recognized (though perhaps we did not say this explicitly) how the particular vision of the relation between the divine, the human, and the natural world associated with biblical theology might have helped make the Shoah possible. Clearly, part of what makes Auschwitz so uniquely horrifying is the highly technological mode of extermination the Nazis put into practice—a technological mode of extermination made possible, in admittedly the very long run, by the biblical view of nature as subject to human will which underlies the scientific world view. Perhaps more important, the degree of instinctual repression associated with ethical monotheism can issue in an intense longing to be free of moral constraint (as Sigmund Freud showed so plainly in his *Moses and Monotheism*). Part of what terrifies about the Nazis is how they unleashed a regressive desire for a world without limitation which, the Bible itself suggests, lies dormant in all of us. Paradoxically, a religion focused on obedience makes radical disobedience a deep temptation.

Rebirth Of The Goddess

Part of what pulled many of us to a goddess focused thealogy was the different understanding of evil we found in archaic goddess traditions. These ancient goddesses, we believed, were imagined as immanent in the world rather than transcendent to it, as identified with all that is, givers of all and takers of all, associated with life and death, feast and famine, and with a recognition that pain and suffering are simply part of the life cycle—not punishment. What we learned from these traditions made us more appreciative of the mystery of the cycles of birth, death, and renewal, and of the interconnectedness of all forms of life.

Some of us (like Marija Gimbutas) found in the Goddess an all-nurturing, all-loving mother, and came to believe that ancient goddess-worshipping cultures were egalitarian, harmonious, and pacific, that it was only with the destruction of these cultures by god-worshipping patriarchal invaders that gender and class oppression and war became part of the human story.

I question this. I see the Goddess (or, as I have always preferred to say, the goddesses) as truly the source of all that is, life and death, good fortune and bad, and therefore—from our human perspective, in relation to *our* hopes and fears—as the good mother and the terrible mother in one. For me, as for Richard Rubenstein:

> A new understanding of God arising out of the return to earth and nature must inevitably confront the issue of the dark divinity.... For the Lord of history there can be no such issue, for all guilt and darkness rests on man's side. This is not so in the religion of nature, insofar as there is a sense of mankind's unity with nature and nature's source, a demonic aspect to reality and divinity must be accepted as an inescapable concomitant to life and existence.[4]

I believe what I have most deeply learned from the goddesses about good and evil is how complexly they are intertwined.

I believe this is true of the goddesses of the Neolithic world explored by Gimbutas, although of course everything we can say about the beliefs and metaphysical views of that world must be based on attempts to reconstruct the meaning of the surviving artifacts, particularly the female figurines which Gimbutas studied with such close attention, with so much human empathy, and so vivid an imagination. Gimbutas herself acknowledged the importance of going back and forth between later and earlier periods and recognized that evidence from classical Greece can supplement and verify our understanding of the appearance and function of the prehistoric goddess. "Written sources pour blood into her veins of stone, clay, bone or gold."[5]

My understanding of ancient goddesses is shaped by those later written sources. To communicate my understanding of how good and evil were imagined in goddess-centered religions I turn to stories told about goddesses with names and histories, goddesses whose myths and rituals we have some access to.

In Greek mythology the most obvious example of the goddess as "all that is" is Gaia, the goddess of the beginning, who is both earth, the earth we walk on and plow and bury our dead in, and the partially anthropomorphized goddess of the earth. She is the parthenogenetic creator of sea and sky, the goddess of volcano and earthquake, of the earth alive and in motion, of birth, growth, change—and thus of death, because resistance to death is resistance to change and to life.

A more dramatic example is the Hindu goddess Kali, a goddess with two faces, the face of the nurturing mother and the face of a fierce cruel demon nourished by the blood of her devotees. To understand Kali's redemptive essence, we have to recognize the simultaneous presence in her of these two faces. She is frightening—*and,* she is the Mother. She embodies all the unwelcome but inescapable ambiguities of human existence, the death of the newborn infant not just of the aged grandparent, the sense of a world gone suddenly out of control, the absurdity of things as they are. Kali cannot be merciful. It is naive to ask that of her, naive to seek to transform her into the Good Mother. As David Kinsley says, "If Kali is mistress, the world is an insane asylum. Can you accept that?"[6] Can you recognize the sacredness in this vision of how things really are? Can you worship the goddess of all that is as it is?

Another powerful example is the Egyptian goddess Sekhmet, the lion-headed daughter of the sun-god Re who is herself associated with the destructive power of the noonday sun. The most important myth about this goddess is a tale of destruction gotten out of hand. Re has aged as Egyptian gods do; he has become senile, incontinent, impotent. When the humans become aware of his weakness and plot against him, hoping to wrest power from the gods, Sekhmet is sent to subdue their rebellion. Initially her purpose is to restore divine order, to recreate the former balance between the gods and humankind, but she gets carried away, becomes bloodthirsty. "When I slay men my heart rejoices," she proclaims. When the other gods see that she seems prepared to annihilate all humankind, they realize that she must somehow be stopped. Finally they come up with a plan. They fill the battlefield with urns of beer mixed with pomegranate juice. Sekhmet lifts one up and gulps its contents. "Ah, more blood," she cries. And greedily turns to the next urn. Soon she has emptied all of them and soon thereafter falls asleep in a drunken stupor. When she awakens, she has come back to her senses.

The dark side of the Greek goddesses is comparatively so muted, so much easier to acknowledge and integrate. Sekhmet reminds us that there are darker energies in the natural world and, by implication, in us, as human, as natural beings. She has helped me to see these impulses as *natural*—not as pure evil, not as satanic, but as part of a whole. I see us as being like her, see our destructive energies as capable of getting as fearfully out of control as did hers. And I mourn what we have done and may yet do. But I also feel such love for our species, and see how it is our *nature,* that which is most distinctive and beautiful and worthy of love about us, our longing to understand, to make, to transform, that has gotten out of hand. I see how closely the good and evil in us (and not only in these goddesses) are intertwined. Somehow the very thing that makes us capable of evil is what is beautiful about us, is the source of our creativity.

Thus it seems to me that what the goddess traditions give us is a *naturalization* of human evil—a seeing it from outside, from a non-anthropocentric perspective, as part of the ebb and flow, the ongoing cycle of creation and destruction, as not unlike earthquake or volcano.

And I believe it is deeply important to be able to move into this perspective, this way of viewing our species.

ReVisioning the Biblical Perspective

Yet I have come to believe that there is also something inadequate about this larger vision, that it is just as important when considering human evil to stay within the human frame, to adopt an anthropocentric perspective. I have come to believe we must also be able to distinguish between evil and misfortune. I am aware of a need to honor my felt sense that the awful suffering that flood, earthquake, or volcanic eruption can cause is significantly different from what happens through human agency, different from those situations where the evil we do one another is the problem, and different from those situations where we recognize ourselves as called upon to contest evil's power over us, in us. And when I feel the need to look at evil in this way, as a human problem, to my surprise I find myself rediscovering the relevance and power of the biblical images.

As many of you know I first turned to the goddesses because of a dream. In the dream I had found myself feeling dislocated, lost, uncentered, and so had done what in waking life at that time I would also have done if overtaken by such feelings. I'd driven toward the desert, first on an interstate, then on a secondary road, and eventually on a dirt road, barely distinguishable from the sands on either side. I'd left the city at dusk, by now it was fully dark. Suddenly I felt a wrench of the wheel and knew immediately that one of my tires had gone flat. I opened the car door and started toward the trunk and then remembered that, alas, I had no spare tire, and recalled that it was a very long time, indeed, since I had passed any other automobiles. But far off in the distance I thought I saw a flickering light and felt it must come from some isolated house where there might be a phone from which I could call for help. So I set out toward the light, but after several moments realized that it was getting no closer and that I was no longer sure it was there at all. I decided that I had better do what I probably should have done at the outset, return to my car and wait for the help that would surely eventually come. But when I turned to do that, I discovered there was no car, there was not even a road, that now I was really lost. Then suddenly from behind an enormous sage bush there appeared a wizened, bearded old man with beautiful blue eyes and a gentle smile. I recognized him immediately, it was Martin Buber, the Jewish theologian about whose work I had written my dissertation. "Can I help you?" he asked. "*No*," I replied, "You and I have been through this before. Now it is time for me to go in search of Her." When I woke from the dream what I remembered most vividly was the assurance with which I had said, "Now it is time for me to go in search of Her." It was those words which led me first to Persephone and then to the other Greek goddesses with whom I've been so deeply involved in the twenty-five years since I had that dream.

At the time of the dream I thought of this turn to the goddesses as a turning away from Buber (and from the biblical mythos so central to his understanding of our human being-here). Only recently have I recognized that in the dream it was only when Buber appeared that I knew how to proceed. And only recently have I come to recognize that my turn to the goddesses was not a rejection of my earlier way but a continuation.

A few months ago I reread Buber's little book, *Good And Evil*, in which he explores what the biblical myths about good and evil, especially some of the tales of Genesis, might have to say to us "latecomers of the spirit" who, as he puts it, have outgrown these myths but are still accessible to them. As I read, I became aware of how although for me the biblical mythos is a broken one with no automatic authority, it is nonetheless still illuminating and challenging. Indeed, in a strange way, this mythos seems more powerful after having been rejected as *the* mythos.

It's as if the biblical god, YHVH, has become a necessary figure in my pantheon, as part of a polytheistic system which needs this upstart young god who claims to be the only one, this god who keeps calling us to be responsible, to turn away from evil, to choose the good. There's a tradition in Greek mythology that Dionysos was a late-appearing god who so clearly represented a form of divine energy with which none of the other gods were associated that the Greeks had to recognize this was, indeed, a god and so had to make room for him in their pantheon. I'm trying to say something similar, that YHVH clearly *is* a god, different from any of the others, and *has* to be recognized, honored, included, not as *the* god, but nonetheless as god.

Somehow taking Auschwitz seriously leads me back to this god, a god for whom the relation to humankind is central not incidental, a god who created us for the sake of our response, who created us as response-able—to him and to one another, a god who wants us to live with one another in love and justice not only to worship him. We now know that during most of the pre-exilic period for kings, priests and the common folk this god was part of a religious system which included other deities.[7] I am led back to *this* YHVH, not to the strict monotheism of the prophets and the postexilic priests and rabbis, not to the omnipotent wholly benevolent Lord of history, not to the notion that suffering is merited punishment—but to the understanding of our human being-here I find implicit in the biblical story of Adam and Eve.

This story suggests that eating of the tree of good and evil, coming to know good and evil, is what puts us outside the garden, outside of childlike innocence, and brings us into history, into the world as we know it. This story sees men and women as created with the freedom to disobey, but not really knowing what that means until afterward, after they *have* disobeyed. As Buber says, the eating seems to be a dreamlike action, rather than a deliberate decision. Only afterwards did they, do we, know ourselves as responsible beings, as response-able—that is, as choosers, deciders. "We humans," Buber says, "are the only beings for whom the real is continually fringed with the possible."[8] Only afterwards do we know ourselves as creatures capable of imaging alternatives, as creatures capable of remembering the past and anticipating the future. Only afterwards do we become aware of the irreversibility of time—and our longing it were not so. Only afterwards are we aware of our mortality, an awareness that seems to be part of the pain of being conscious beings—and aware of our impossible longing to return to Eden, where one just *is* good without having to choose to be good and where goodness and happiness coincide. As Buber puts it, this story reminds us of our longing for shelter—and of our discovery that there is none.

What I learn from this biblical story is what I have also learned from Freud, from the Freud who woke to discover "I am Oedipus," the Freud who discovered as still alive in himself (and he believed in all of us) a profound inextinguishable longing for the unconditional love we feel we knew to begin with, at the breast or in the womb. The Freud who speaks to us of that voice in us which cries, "I want all of her, I want all of her, all to myself." The Freud who also knew of the deep murderous resentment I therefore feel toward anyone who intrudes between me and her, between me and the fullness of love, of being fully known and fully embraced, I imagine I once had and still long for. Freud also saw how the avoidance, the denial, of our mortality and the refusal to recognize our finitude, to accept limitation leads to aggression against others. "He should die, so I don't have to."

Similarly, Buber saw radical evil as arising when our longing to be the only one, to have it all go my way, to deny any limits, leads to denial of the personhood of others. He saw how our resentment and fear of others, of our dependence on them, leads us to treat them as "It"s not "Thou"s.

The Holocaust is an extreme example—but we all know this temptation.

A temptation which is highlighted in the later stories of Genesis which, as I related last year, return again and again to the theme of brotherly rivalry, the theme of wanting to be *the* one, the only one. How right, sadly, that the story of Adam and Eve should be followed immediately by the story of Cain and Abel.

These brothers are the first fully human beings; the first born is the first murderer. *This* is us. I also spoke last year of how Genesis ends with a scene of forgiveness and thus witnesses to a celebration of the moments of reconciliation, forgiveness, harmony, and peace that do occur—even though there will still be later moments of betrayal, conflict, and suffering.

So let me try to say where all this leads me:

I do not believe in the possibility of eliminating human evil. I see it as too closely tied to the kind of creature we are.

But I believe—I hope—we can move to not being overtaken by it, not succumb to what, following Buber, I call radical evil.

I believe this will be possible only if we acknowledge the reality of the human capacity for evil and especially its power in us.

I agree with Buber that evil is not in the soul but in the between—in the relation between the self and the human world. Evil happens as occurrence, as event. It's not doing evil but deliberately persisting in it that is the problem. There is a difference between missing the way and opposing it.

Because time *is* irreversible, there's a sense in which guilt is ineradicable. Yet I believe there is nevertheless a way forward, through acknowledgment of the real wounds I've inflicted, through recognition of my need for forgiveness, and through reparation, active efforts to heal, to reconnect with the particular others I've injured.

I also believe that my recognition of this need to try to heal expresses a recognition of my shared humanity with the one I've harmed—and thus an awareness that the other participates in the same primary longings and fears which underlie my own evil. And this leads to my recognizing *their* need for forgiveness as like unto my own.

Only thus, only through acknowledging both our real capacity to do evil to one another and our capacity to try to heal, to repair, will there be a future—for ourselves—and here my goddess perspective reappears—and just as importantly, for all else that lives on this earth with us.

Notes

1. Richard L. Rubenstein, *After Auschwitz,* 2nd ed. (Baltimore: The Johns Hopkins University Press, 1992) 200.

2. Richard L. Rubenstein, *After Auschwitz,* 1st ed. (Indianapolis: Bobbs-Merrill, 1966) 80, 68–70. The essays from which these quotations are taken are

included in the second 1992 edition of Rubenstein's book; in the new preface he says he now feels greater empathy for those who have reaffirmed traditional Jewish faith in the face of the Holocaust and modifies his earlier affirmation of a form of Jewish paganism as an appropriate response to the Holocaust. He sees in retrospect that this affirmation may have seemed to encourage a kind of literalistic attachment to the land of Israel that has brought some fundamentalist Zionists into conflict with Palestinians in a way Rubenstein had never intended. What he had meant was a "form of nature religion in which *all men and women understand themselves as children of Earth,*" xiii (Rubenstein's italics). He also writes, "Today I no longer regard the cosmos as 'cold, silent, unfeeling.' At the very least, insofar as man is a part of the cosmos and is capable of love as well as hate, the cosmos cannot be said to be entirely cold and silent…. Today I would balance the elements of creation and love more evenly with those of destruction and hate than was possible in 1966," 172. "The dialectical-mystical elements in my thinking have endured; the pagan element has proven less durable," 174.

3. Archibald MacLeish, *J.B.* (Boston, 1958) 21.

4. Rubenstein, 1966, 140.

5. Marija Gimbutas, *The Gods and Goddesses of Old Europe* (Berkeley: University of California Press, 1982) 197.

6. David Kinsley, *The Sword and the Flute* (Berkeley: University of California Press, 1982) 131, 135.

7. Cf. Mark S. Smith, *The Early History of God: Yahweh and Other Deities in Ancient Israel* (New York: Harper & Row, 1990).

8. Martin Buber, *Good and Evil* (New York: Harper, 1953) 125.

5

Freud's Mythology of Soul

This is a day dedicated to a celebration of Alan Sparks' twenty-five years at SDSU. In preparing to be part of that honoring I've been remembering how Alan and I both came to SDSU in the fall of 1974, he to take a position in the Graduate Division, I for a one semester fill-in position while Allan Anderson was on leave. Neither Alan Sparks nor I would have imagined then that for most of the rest of the next quarter century one or the other of us would be chairing the Religious Studies Department.

As I've been remembering the fall of 1974 I've also remembered that it was that fall that I was installed as the first woman president of the American Academy of Religion and thus that it was then that I gave my presidential address on Sigmund Freud and the Greek Mythological Tradition—an address, I recall, that dismayed many of my feminist friends who couldn't believe that I would choose to use this long-awaited occasion to speak on Freud, that arch misogynist. I admit it's been comforting over the years to see how one by one most of those who were so disappointed then have come to look upon Freud more as friend than as foe. In any case, remembering that occasion led me to think it might be appropriate to use this fifth Christine Downing Lecture to go back to Freud and see what I'd have to say about him now.

I see this as an occasion also to honor the 100th anniversary of the publication of Freud's *Interpretation of Dreams*—which though it bore the date 1900 was actually published in 1899. Freud deliberately misdated the book because he had the chutzpah to assume his was a book that belonged to the new century. A chutzpah that in retrospect seems well justified. For as Paul Robinson wrote in a recent review of the current Freud exhibit at the Library of Congress which gives voice to Freud's detractors as well as his admirers, "We may safely pronounce him the dominant intellectual presence of our century."

Of course in this short hour I can't do all of Freud. So I have chosen a perspective very close to the one of 25 years ago, and one that seems singularly appropriate to this religious studies lecture: Freud's Mythology of Soul.

I want to begin by acknowledging that what I'll be sharing is *my* Freud. There are, of course, many ways of reading Freud, and I would say that none of them are true, none represent *the* valid reading. Freud has been read as both jailer and liberator, as scientist and artist, realist and romantic. There's an enlightenment Freud and a post-modern Freud. Many seem tempted to identify Freud with but one of these positions, whereas I see Freud's texts as "over-determined" and am persuaded they cannot be reduced to one level of significance, one interpretation. After all, to look for latent meanings in the manifest surface of Freud's texts, to discover the under-texts, is to participate in a mode of reading which he himself taught us in his interpretations of dreams, parapraxes, symptoms, and literature. To honor the tensions, the contradictions in Freud's thought—that, I believe, is where the juice lies.

My reading of Freud thus seeks to allow him to say as much as he can, to teach me as much as he can, aims at allowing him to enrich, challenge, deepen my thinking. I've been reading and rereading Freud (and much of the secondary literature) for almost 40 years now. I keep rereading Freud because I have found in him language for what matters most to me (although, of course, I realize other languages may do so more fully for you).

My reading of Freud is undoubtedly in large measure shaped by my having come to Freud from Jung. So that my reading of Freud is in some significant ways a Jungian one; not one that reduplicates Jung's reading of Freud (which I regard as distorted) but simply that of someone who knew Jung's work first and reads Freud in a way that emphasizes the poetic, metaphorical, mythic dimension of his psychology. I see myself as someone whose thinking has been deeply influenced by both. Together they have parented my vision of my self, my vision of the human soul.

I knew Jung's work first—as we know the mother long before we know the father—and still experience him as mother of my soul. In my early twenties he gave me myself, a vital, nourishing relationship to my inner life, my dreams and imaginal capabilities. I continue to recognize this gift as an unequivocal blessing. But there was a sense in which Jung for me was too much like a soft pillow; some spark necessary to my own creative activity was missing. And that I found when a few years later I turned to Freud—whom I have learned from by contending with and rebelling against, as one does with a father. In the intervening years I have learned that my vision still needs to be both mothered and fathered, that I remain unwilling to respond to the imperative: You must choose between them, between the divorced parents.

So today I want to talk about Freud, my Freud, and to focus on his understanding of the psyche, the soul. I would like to show how because Freud viewed the body as the dwelling place of soul, he found that to speak of the soul, of its deepest longings and most profound terror, is to speak of the body, of sexuality and death. And that to speak of the body as the soul knows it, is to speak metaphorically, imaginatively, mythically—to speak of Oedipus and Narcissus, of Eros and Death. I want to look at the role these three myths play in the development of Freud's understanding of the soul—how he finds that behind the myth of Oedipus lurks the myth of Narcissus and behind that the myth of the eternal struggle between Death and Love.

But first I need to make clear that Freud does speak of the soul. It seems to me signally important to recognize the degree to which his lifelong love of classical culture shaped Freud's way of understanding the psyche. He spoke often of his schoolboy delight in Greek poetry and philosophy, and as an adolescent dreamt of becoming an archaeologist. He was reading Schliemann's account of the excavations at Troy and Mycenae while writing *Interpretation of Dreams* and by then understood himself as engaged in an archaeology of the soul. As an adult he was an avid collector of ancient near eastern antiquities and in a letter to Fliess spoke of the figurines gracing his writing desk as his "gods." This enduring immersion in the ancient world led him to be attuned to the etymological overtones of psychological terms in a way we Americans aren't. So that we hear as professional jargon what he heard as having mythological resonance.

Rightly to apprehend Freud's logos of the psyche it seems to me essential to know that he consistently used the word *Seele* where the English translation gives us "mind," "mental structure," or "mental organization." *Seele* is the German word for soul and Freud meant by *Seele* the psyche of Greek mythology and philosophy. In his invaluable book, *Freud and Man's Soul*, Bruno Bettelheim says that for Freud *Seele* refers to "the fragile insubstantial essence of the self which needs to be approached gently and with love." Freud's *Seele* is the Psyche of the Hellenistic fairy tale about Psyche and Eros which describes how the soul's journey to self is motivated by love of an other for whom one does what one couldn't quite do on one's own and which relates how Psyche had to journey to the underworld to become psyche, become herself.

Freud's *Seele* is the soul of psychology not of religion. Freud was not religious in any conventional sense, not a theist and most emphatically not a monotheist. His *Seele* is *Psyche* not *pneuma,* not the transcending spirit but the embodied soul. It is the soul of Hebrew scripture, of Genesis, not of Christian theology. Not that aspect of us which is literally immortal, but what enlivens us while we are alive. The soul is the breath of life. It enters at birth, leaves at death. It connects us to the world, each time we breathe in or out, and enables us to be speaking beings. Soul is in a sense a metaphor, a myth. It has no physical correlate, though we can't help but imagine it spatially. It dwells in the body but can't be located anatomically. I can't help but recall the ancient Greek view which located psyche in the diaphragm, in one of the hollows, the empty spaces, of the body.

For Freud to speak of the soul, of its deepest longings and most profound terror, is to speak of the body. He sought a language for the self that takes seriously that we are embodied souls, ensouled bodies. He sought to give voice to the speech of the soul (*psyche-logos*) rather than speak objectifyingly about it, and discovered (in his work with women suffering from hysteria) that the soul speaks through the body, that the psyche uses the language of the body to express itself. He learned to hear somatic symptoms as language, not as gibberish but as expressions of an otherwise silenced soul, learned to read symptoms as symbols. "Symptoms are like mythological figures," he writes, "all powerful guests from an alien world, immortal beings intruding into the turmoil of mortal life."

I believe Freud was able to enter so deeply into the hysterical imagination because he in a sense participates in it. He, too, has a predilection for body metaphors, for speaking of the soul through the language of the body. His favorite figure of speech is synecdoche, the taking of a part for whole. Thus oral and anal become ways of talking about fundamental life-orientations, not just food or feces; castration anxiety and penis envy become ways of talking about some of the most fundamental concerns associated with our gendered existence. We wholly misunderstand Freud if we fail to hear these terms as metaphor.

Yet it is essential that we recognize that Freud doesn't take the body literally, as his rejection of medical training as appropriate preparation for becoming an analyst ought to make evident. "The theory of the drives is our mythology," he writes to Einstein, and *drive—"Trieb"* not "Instinct"—is indeed the irreducible, ultimately self-explicable term, the "god-term," of Freud's psychology. This choice of language is intended to emphasize the ultimate unity of soma and psyche, body and soul. Drive is need become wish, energy become meaning, physiological instinct transformed into mental activity.

For Freud, then, to speak of the soul is to speak of the body, and thus neces-sarily of sexuality and death. His insistence on the inextricable enmeshment of body and soul leads to a logos of the psyche which takes seriously our sexuality, our mortality, and our inescapable involvements with other desiring/acting embodied beings, with family and with society. Long before he begins to speak of Eros and Death, Freud responded to sexuality and death as numinous, as sacred. Though he claimed a deafness to the mystical, it is evident that he felt the tran-scendent here.

Our sexuality is not only the meeting place of body and soul but also the meeting place of self and other. Freud speaks of the importance of the human move to face-to-face intercourse, of a lovemaking which involves not only the connection of body to body, but of eye to eye, soul to soul. He sees our sexuality as taking us out of ourselves, beyond an intra-psychic psychology. We are directed toward world and particularly to human others—*and* we are narcissistic, would often wish to deny, to escape, this interdependence.

Freud's understanding of sexuality was always transliteral, always meant more than genitality, more than normal, adult, heterosexual, reproduction-directed sex. He saw human sexuality as connected to our capacity for metaphorical think-ing, for symbolization, for myth-making. His awe of the sexual is also awe of our imaginative capacities. There's a two-way vector of interpretation: culture means sexual energy but also human sexuality means the possibility of culture.

He reminds us of the unique features of human sexuality, especially of the malleability which is such a central feature of human sexuality. The nonperiodic aspect of our sexuality, our continuous openness to arousal, means we have to learn to choose, to delay, to substitute, and this ability to substitute is at the heart of sublimation, of symbolization. Arousal can be diverted to what we'd still call sexual: not now, later; not here, there; not her, him—or to what might be more difficult to recognize as such, to a poem, for example, which may not even be about my longing for her but about waves crashing on the shore.

We learn from Freud that we are more sexual than we had hitherto sus-pected—and more symbolic. He encourages us to celebrate our capacity for sub-limation (which he likens to alchemical magic)—to take conscious delight in writing the poem instead of fucking the stranger, in being able to love again when the first love is irretrievably lost—at the same time that we mourn what once was or could never be, encourages us to honor our exuberant inventiveness, the resil-ience of our imagination.

But Freud's mythology of sexuality is never a salvific myth; he never suggests that sexuality could save us, fulfill us. From his perspective we have both defined sexuality too narrowly—and asked too much of it. He sees our sexuality as an expression of our deepest human longings—our longings for full expression and full acceptance, for physical closeness and emotional intimacy—and sees how our sexuality is always a wounded sexuality. He aims to help us recognize the perversity of normality, of adult socially-approved sexuality—the cost of being cut off from our rebellious, regressive, unconscious sexuality, from our bisexuality, from a full-body sensuality. He seeks to remind us how in the beginning sensuality and affection are closely intertwined, and to help us recognize how easily, how frequently, they become separated. He sees how our sexuality seems always to carry with it an impossible longing for complete satisfaction. He speaks of the sadness that seems always to follow upon coitus and believes that in love-making we are always really looking for the first love, the mother, and even further back to our enclosure in her womb, to that time when there was no separation between self and other.

For Freud to speak of the soul or of the body is always to speak of being wounded, of suffering. Ernest Jones wrote that Freud "taught us that the secrets of the human soul were to be apprehended only in connection with suffering; through being able to suffer oneself and thus entering into contact with the suffering of others." For Freud the starting point of any depth psychology was pathology—*pathos-logos*—the speech in us of that in us which seems to happen to us, our passivity, our feeling, our suffering; that which hurts and is vulnerable, what is anxious and destructive. He believed this pathological aspect has its own voice and wishes, longs to be heard and understood, that we all suffer, are all conflicted.

To speak adequately of this suffering, he learned, is to speak mythically. I see Freud's discovery of the living reality of myth as marking the real beginning of psychoanalysis. This discovery grew out of his own experience, his self-analysis. I am my most difficult patient, he told Fliess, and the one from whom I've learned the most. Freud (like Jung) had the chutzpah to assume the archetypal, the universal, the mythic significance of his own experience. He believed he had discovered through the exploration of his own psyche clues to what is true of the deepest experience of all of us.

His self-analysis was provoked by the death of his father, a loss which issued in a sustained period of depression, introversion, and of being flooded by dreams and new insights. His father's death seems to have functioned like a "shamanic wound." Until then the unconscious was something that others had, an important force in the life of his hysterical patients but not really in the psyches of normal persons like himself. His grief, his suffering, his discovery of the ambivalent feelings he had toward a father he had thought he loved unreservedly, brought Freud into touch with his own unconscious.

The starting point was suffering. His father died in October, 1896; almost exactly a year later Freud had the dream from which he awoke knowing: "I am Oedipus." (Not: "I have an Oedipus complex.") For Freud "Oedipus" was not an illustration or clever designation for an insight which might have been articulated otherwise, but the medium of discovery. Indeed, his understanding of the oedipal continued to unfold for decades. He came to mean by "Oedipus" everything associated with the hero of Sophocle's *Oedipus Tyrannos*—and later also by *Oedipus at Colonus*.

He especially wanted to suggest that he had discovered as still alive in himself—and he believed in all of us—a profound inextinguishable longing for the unconditional love we knew at the breast, in the womb. Pointing to the persistence in us of incestuous wish and parricidal longing was his way of calling our attention to that voice still alive in us which cries: I want her; I want all of her—all to myself. And to our deep murderous resentment of anyone who intrudes between us and her, between us and the fullness of love we imagine we once had and still long for.

Self and other—self and lack—appear together. To be a person is to be wanting, in need, wish-driven, lacking. We become aware of being persons, of being a self through the discovery of our insufficiency, of our helplessness. Freud sees the Oedipus myth as making visible the primacy of desire—and the inevitability of its frustration, the inescapable connection between sexuality and the unattainable, the pain of being human. The loss of that imagined blissful first love issues in unavowable grief and rage, unappeased longing, unmitigated terror. Having lost our first love, we always feel threatened by loss. Indeed, the knowledge of the loss somehow precedes the knowledge of the love. (We know Eden as Eden only after the gates have closed behind us.)

Incest and parricide are thus not to be understood literally, and yet they are connected to actual experience, bodily experience, childhood experience. Thus we misread Freud—make him into a Jungian—if we understand incest and parricide as "only metaphor." Freud also meant by "Oedipus" the commitment to self-knowledge (even when painful) exemplified by Oedipus's persistence in his search to discover the true identity of the one whose murderous deed had brought death to his city. (It is actually this aspect that is emphasized in *Interpretation of Dreams*.)

The Oedipus myth also shows how the story never begins with us; psychologically we enter into a world already there, a world of others, become ourselves in

response to their desires, their fears. As Oedipus's life was shaped by his parents'
fears, by the curse laid on his father—and in turn his dying curse fatefully
impacts his children's lives.

And in his later years of suffering from the unremitting pain of his cancer,
Freud identified with the blind exiled Oedipus utterly dependent on being led by
his daughter Antigone—as Freud had become dependent on his daughter Anna
to insert each morning and then remove each night the prosthesis that separated
his oral and nasal cavities, and to deliver his speeches when he, Sigmund, Sigmund, the victorious mouth, no longer could. "My Anna, my Antigone," he
called her. In those years he identified with the Oedipus who had come to terms
with his finitude, the Oedipus who was ready to die.

I am Oedipus, he said. Fully to know myself is to acknowledge this identification. And in saying this he was rediscovering what myth-oriented cultures have
always affirmed: we find our identity through discovering a mythic model. Freud
learned that to be a self is to be others, we become ourselves through a series of
identifications. Though there is no question that the myth of Oedipus has particular power for him, almost as important to Freud were his identifications with
several biblical figures—Jacob, Joseph, and Moses—and with other classical
mythic figures—Psyche and Eros, as we've already noted, and Narcissus.

It was Havelock Ellis not Freud who first introduced the term narcissism into
psychology, but in Freud's use the term became much more than simply a fancy
word for auto-eroticism or masturbation. He brings some of the full richness of
Ovid's telling of the myth back into psychology, particularly the close association
of narcissism and death. Ovid's Narcissus is a beautiful youth who rejects the love
of the nymph Echo and of many male admirers, one of whom implores the gods,
"May he too fall in love with another and be unable to gain his loved one." So at
the edge of a barely moving stream Narcissus falls in love with his own reflected
image, unaware that it is his own. Only when he discovers this does he fall into
immobilizing despair—and not knowing whether to woo or be wooed, slowly
wastes away and dies.

Narcissus in the myth is someone who takes his own reflection for another,
who can't distinguish between self and other. As, so Freud believes, none of us
can at the beginning, when enmeshed in what he calls primary narcissism, that
early pre-psychical, pre-verbal stage in which there is no self and no other, a stage
which exists only in memory, in fantasy, only for the imagination—only afterwards. Consciousness, as we noted earlier, begins with the experience of separation and loss. Self and other are co-created—and thus arises the twin possibility

of self-love and other-love. The Oedipus myth expresses the soul meaning of one, Narcissus of the other.

Some of the originally undifferentiated libido is directed to the self, some to others. Consciousness entails a departure from primary narcissism, a transfer of some of the love that might be directed toward ourselves to another. Often we may try to in a sense have it both ways, to love someone who reminds us of ourselves, or of our earlier selves, or our ideal selves. We are also likely to over-estimate the beloved to make up for the forfeited self-love—and to need to be loved back to recover the forfeited self-love. And when we aren't loved, there is always an enormous temptation to entirely withdraw libido from the outer world and thus fall into what Freud calls "secondary narcissism."

Narcissism thus represents an earlier, more primary stage than Oedipal love; it arises in response to the separation between what is not yet an ego and not yet an object, out of longing to deny the loss, the dependency, the neediness, to claim a self-sufficiency. Our initial turn to another expresses our impossible longing for an other to give us back that lost wholeness. It is really an expression of fusion longing, expresses a desire to *be* not to *have*.

Only after the full acknowledgment of the loss, only after what Freud calls the work of mourning, does there really arise the possibility of turning to other as other, as a genuinely separate object with its own desires which are not just for me. Only, we might say, when we acknowledge the existence of a rival, admit that the mother does not exist only in relation to us, only as we enter the Oedipal world, does the possibility of real loving, of Eros, emerge.

Narcissism is an illusion; we are in a world with others; we are not self-sufficient, we are not the world. And thus narcissism is death. Freud quotes Heine: "We must learn to love in order not to fall ill." But it is also true that the narcissistic longings never die. For we all long to return to that earlier fantasized world where self and other were one, all long to believe that separation is not the ultimate truth. As Julia Kristeva puts it, "the lover is a narcissist with an object." Eros is the long way round back to narcissism, to death—an *aufhebung* of narcissism, its overcoming *and* its continuation by other means.

From the time of that dream from which he awoke knowing "I am Oedipus," Freud knew that to speak adequately of the psyche requires recourse to mythological and metaphorical language. In the writings of his last years the figures of the twin Titans, Eros and Death, come to loom as large as had the figure of Oedipus earlier on. In her *Tribute to Freud* the poet H.D. who was a patient of Freud's in the early 1930s wrote, "Eros and Death—these two were the chief subjects, indeed the only subjects—of the Professor's eternal preoccupation." And as he told her, "My psychology lays the basis for a very grave philosophy."

During the last two decades of his life Freud's emphasis shifts from the psychological to the metapsychological and to the period in our lives where the mother is the most important figure for both boys and girls, a period Freud sees as equivalent to the Minoan-Mycenaean period in Greek history when goddesses were more important than gods. During this time death also became an ever more important theme in Freud's writing. Among contributing factors we might name the painful breaks with Adler and Jung, the outbreak of the First World War which he saw as making evident the costs of the repression of aggression and death wish, the deaths of one of his daughters and of a beloved grandson soon after the war's end, and his own cancer which served as a constant reminder of his own oncoming death.

As Death becomes an ever more important theme, Freud comes to speak of Eros, the cosmic life principle, rather than of sexuality. It is important, however, that we recognize that this does not represent a move from body to spirit, but rather an even deeper contemplation of the meaning of our embodiment and finitude. Freud has become deeply aware of how precarious our love of life is, how there is something inside us which works against that in us which wants, against that in us which is turned to the future, to others, to the new, against what he now calls Eros.

He looks upon Eros and Death as two primal powers, as cosmological not just psychological energies, forces that are at work in us, through us, and in the whole outer world. He speaks of them as twin brothers, engaged in a dramatic struggle with one another and sometimes in so close an embrace that we cannot distinguish between them. To speak of them as mythological figures is to engage in an age-old human way of figuring the most powerful forces at work in the universe. Freud does not call upon us to worship these Titans but simply to acknowledge their power—and to remember that they do not constitute a moral dichotomy. We should not fall into the trap of regarding Eros as good or Death as bad.

Freud's Eros is, of course, not the childish Cupid of popular imagination. He is the Eros of Apuleius and of Plato—and of Hesiod and the Orphics, the creative principle which is the source of all being, all life. Freud clearly distinguishes Eros from what he calls "oceanic feeling," from fusion longing, which Freud viewed as regressive, narcissistic, directed by death longing. His Eros is clearly an active "masculine" figure, an energy directed outward, toward real, particular others. Not to all, that would be fusion longing once again, but to an ever widening, more inclusive circle of others. His Eros is one of the parents of civilization, as

Auden puts it, the "builder of cities." Freud sees civilization, communal existence, as dependent on libidinal attachments not just on the containment of
aggression: society is based on love *and* our fear and hatred of others. We want
and resent society; it fulfills and frustrates us; we accept it and rebel against it;
part of us adapts to the restrictions it demands, part doesn't.

The twin brother of Eros is Death. Freud never calls this figure Thanatos, the
name of the minor Greek god who carries us to the underworld, nor Persephone
or Hades, but simply: *Death*. Early on Freud had focused on the importance of
overcoming the repression and literalization of sexuality; later he comes to
emphasize the importance of overcoming the repression and literalization of
death.

Death, as Freud speaks of it, is of course a psychical and not simply a biologi-
cal reality. He suggests that narcissism may be the most intimate and archaic
expression of the death drive. The goal of all life is death, he tells us, with ever
more complicated detours. Death is something we both long for and fear. He
associates death fear with our fears of the unknown, the uncanny, the unconscious; with our fears of vulnerability and passivity; our fears of not being loved,
of being abandoned, of not loving. Death wish is associated with all in us that is
pulled toward repetition, inertia, regression; all that longs for a tension-free existence, for Nirvana resolution, completion; the voices in us that cry "leave me
alone, let me have my way, don't make me change; let me stay a child, let me
return to the womb." Death wish shows itself in our longing to be immortal, to
be remembered, our longing not to die. This is a paradox that Nietzsche also
articulated: the wish not to die is itself a death wish, as is all resistance to change,
to movement, that is, to life.

When denied death-fear and death-wish both become destructive, become
aggression. Again Freud reminds us of our resentful hatred of anything that
intrudes between me and that longed-for peace, that reminds me of my incom-
pleteness, my wanting, my separation from the all. But remember: death is not
the enemy. The death drive is not bad; it represents a given direction of the soul.
Freud hopes to help us recognize the importance of accepting this as part of who
we are, of learning to bear the conflicts within us, of curing our demand for cure,
for resolution, of coming to view conflict as enduring and enlivening. But, then,
that's Eros's view. Death itself might say: we need to honor also that in us which
continues to want happiness, resolution, fulfillment.

In the early 1930s, as Nazism was becoming more and more powerful, Freud
saw a world more and more dominated by Death—and saw how our fear of
Death leads to its gaining more and more power over us. Yet he ends *Civilization*

and Its Discontents, what Adam Phillips calls "his great elegy for happiness," not with words of despair, and of course not with words of easy cheap consolation, but with what comes as close to a prayer as we are ever likely to find in Freud: "But now it is to be hoped that the other of the two heavenly powers, eternal Eros, will make an effort to assert himself in the struggle with his equally immortal adversary." This evocation of hope, of Eros in the light of, not denial of, Death, brings to my mind the last stanzas of the poem, "In Memory of Freud," that W.H. Auden wrote a few month after Freud's death in 1939:

> But he would have us remember most of all
> to be enthusiastic over the night,
>> not only for the sense of wonder
> it alone has to offer, but also
>
> because it needs our love.
>
> Our rational voice is dumb. Over his grave
> the household of Impulse mourns one dearly loved:
>> sad is Eros, builder of cities,
> and weeping, anarchic Aphrodite.

6

Revisiting the Goddesses

I seem to be in a retrospective mood, perhaps that's a crone's privilege. I remember that years ago the American Academy of Religion (or perhaps it was the Society for Biblical Literature) at its annual meetings would invite a prominent scholar to reflect on "How My Mind Has Changed." What I'm doing here is not exactly that, but it is along those lines.

It's twenty years now since I finished my book *The Goddess,* twenty-five since I had the dream in which I found myself "going in search of HER," the dream that eventually issued in the book. It's important to me to remember how long ago this was: It is still so vivid—and in another sense it sometimes seems that the dreamer was almost another woman.

I soon discovered that my search for Her was part of a turn to goddesses by many women at more or less the same time, all initially quite unaware of one another. I'm struck by how little we knew to begin with and by how important it seemed. (I remember teaching my first Goddess class here at SDSU in the spring of 1978—how few resources there were, how we had to make it up as we went along, how much we all cared.) I remember how to begin with we women—Merlin Stone, Charlene Spretnak, Starhawk, Z Budapest, Carol Christ, myself—looked upon ourselves as all part of the same movement. Only gradually did we come to recognize our differences and it took even longer before we could talk about them honestly, critically, and yet respectfully.

Prehistoric Goddesses

Many, perhaps most, of those initially drawn to goddesses were drawn to the prehistoric, prepatriarchal goddesses—and thus deeply influenced by the pioneering work of Marija Gimbutas, as made available through her 1974 *Gods and Goddesses of Old Europe* (retitled in 1982 as *Goddesses and Gods of Old Europe)* and later in her other books, *Language of the Goddess, Civilization of the Goddess.* They

67

felt, as Starhawk put it, that Gimbutas like other great artists has taught us how to *see*. Our response expresses "our felt need for a spirituality that puts earth at the center, that honors women as well as men, that recognizes the sacred authority of the body and that venerates the interconnectedness of all life."[1] Some often seemed to use Gimbutas's inferences as facts, as evidence that patriarchy, war, competitiveness, social hierarchy are recent historical developments. Riane Eisler, for example, in her *The Chalice and the Blade* made clear that her real concern was with the *future*, with *choices* now to be made, and that the prehistory gives us a sense of *possibilities,* a sense that male dominance and violence are not inevitable.

I think it was important to many of us that Gimbutas was a "real" archaeologist, a digger as well as an interpreter. I have always loved the image of Gimbutas finding these evidences of the goddess in the earth, the literalness of re-emergence. I honor her affirmation of the possibility of reconstructing what these artifacts meant to their makers and users and her willingness to risk inferring how they might relate to ritual and belief, to the psycho-social dynamic that inspired their production. "If you do not have vision," she said, "if you are not a poet or an artist, you cannot see much."[2] And I find it worth remembering that she acknowledged the importance of going back and forth between later and earlier eras, that she regarded evidences drawn from literate and preliterate cultures as mutually illuminating. "Written sources." she affirmed, "pour blood into her veins of stone, clay, bone or gold."[3]

Most of you are probably familiar with the central role played in her work of ceramic and stone female figurines excavated at worship sites and graves and with her thesis that these figurines represent divine not human beings, feminine generative not erotic power, that they are *representations of the goddess.* Her books are full of deeply moving illustrations of these ancient sculptures, illustrations which beautifully communicate the rich variety of their forms: Some are fat with pronounced buttocks or bellies or breasts or with exposed pudenda, others are narrow hipped with tiny breasts, folded arms, rigidly posed. Some are nude, some fully clothed, some masked. Some are pregnant, some represented in a squatting, birthgiving position. Some seem more androgynous, with female bodies and phallus shaped heads.

Despite this diversity, Gimbutas views them all as aspects of One Great Goddess. (Perhaps this is easier because these preliterate cultures could leave us no specific names to help us differentiate among them.) Gimbutas assumes that She is really One—the great variety of forms reveal the many different facets of one power, one basic belief: that the female embodies the principle of creativity. The Goddess is the Creator of all that is, the parthenogenetic source of all life. She is the giver of crafts and wisdom, the teacher of horticulture and writing. The main themes of this ancient goddess religion, Gimbutas tells us, center on the mystery of birth, death, renewal and the interconnectedness of all forms of life.

The interpretation of the female figurines later led Gimbutas to interpret animal and hybrid human-animal figurines (most of which seem to be older than the wholly human ones) as also representing the energy of the goddess. She is gifted at helping us understand how bulls, caterpillars, bees, butterflies, snakes, scarabs, toads, turtles, hedgehogs, bears, pigs, vultures and owls all could have been viewed as embodying one aspect or another of the goddess's creative or transformative power.

Gimbutas also put forward deductions about the culture (about the social structure not only the religion) which produced this art. It was, she said, a matrilineal, matrifocal, sedentary, unstratified village culture. There was gender-based division of labor but no ranking along male/female lines. She believed that females supervised the rituals and made the sacred art. Their social existence was harmonious, pacific. "What were they like, our ancestors? They were like us, only happy."

In the work of her last years Gimbutas moved from her focus on the Neolithic period to including the Paleolithic; she came to see goddess religion as beginning 25,000 years ago, as representing the earliest form of religion, in place long before the beginnings of horticulture. She found goddess symbolism in the most ancient geometric art. Long before the appearance of the anthropomorphic or the theriomorphic forms whose language she had learned to "read" earlier, the essentials of goddess religion were already present. Not too surprisingly the degree of continuity she found between the Paleolithic and the Neolithic, the way she found vulvas in every V and saw every V, W, X, Y and Z as a goddess symbol is the aspect of her work which has been most questioned.

Gimbutas was always relatively reticent about the meaning of all this for us. She does say that given how long this religious system was in place it inevitably left indelible imprints on psyche. Occasionally she spoke of her sense of its continued relevance. In articulating her conviction of the absolute necessity of our recovering a sense of the equal value of the masculine and the feminine and of the sacred value of earth, she says: "We could learn much about both from the culture of Old Europe…. The knowledge of Old Europe may affect our vision of the past as well as our sense of potential for the present and the future. We must refocus our collective memory. The necessity for this has never been greater as we discover that the path of 'progress' is extinguishing the very conditions for life on earth."[4]

The tendency among those who examine Gimbutas's work seems to be to reject it completely, vehemently, or to applaud it uncritically. Few have as nuanced a response as Naomi Goldenberg, who questions Gimbutas when she says "The Life-Giving Goddess of Old Europe often manifests as a waterbird" and says she wishes she had instead said that waterbird figures may have been understood as representing sacred life-giving energy. Goldenberg adds that she thinks a thoughtful critic might conclude, "Although I find Gimbutas's notion about a highly evolved thealogy of the Goddess in Old Europe difficult to accept, I see her descriptive phenomenology of many artifacts as plausible."[5]

Most scholars seem to agree about the preponderance of female figures among the artifacts found at Neolithic archaeological sites—though some question Gimbutas's too easy dismissal of the significance of the male figurines and believe Gimbutas too readily interprets figures of unidentifiable gender as female, as she also tends to classify as female what others might call hermaphroditic forms, the ones with phallic heads.

Some still question whether the female figures are necessarily goddesses; that is, they question the cosmological significance Gimbutas attaches to them. Obviously, it all depends on what we mean by "goddess." What connotations does using this term lead us to associate with these figurines? Would we be comfortable using the term "goddess" to refer to localized beings, limited in power, seen only in relation to limited particular functions? It may be that some of these small statues were used primarily in connection with female initiation rites or marriage rites, as birth magic, or as part of an ancestor cult.

Some bless, some question, the assurance with which Gimbutas moves from the artifacts to deductions about social organization and beliefs. Despite general agreement that Neolithic societies were relatively egalitarian, nonpatriarchal, and pacific, Gimbutas is sometimes accused of having too Edenic, too romantic, a view of Neolithic culture, of presenting us with the newest version of the old Noble Savage fantasy. She is seen as perhaps also having too romantic a view of a horticultural as contrasted with hunter-gatherer societies—a view which ignores the violence of animal domestication and how for farmers wild things are the enemy of the farm, how farmers battle weeds and pests and predators.[6]

Though many accept Gimbutas's thesis about the veneration accorded women in the Neolithic world because of the major roles they played in plant cultivation and animal domestication, in weaving and pottery-making, others question her claim that women held dominant or even equal political power and her assumption that the evidences of goddess worship imply that religious art and ritual were in the hands of women. The images might have been made by men, they say; might always have expressed men's relation to the feminine.

Gimbutas's insistence that invaders were responsible for the transition from the old goddess religion to the more patriarchal religious and political systems of the Iron Age represents to some an unwarranted villainizing of IndoEuropean invaders. Colin Renfrew, for example, believes that the spread of IndoEuropean culture and language proceeded not by warfare but by the spread of farming, and claims that archaeology shows no evidence of the kind of dramatic migration and overthrow posited by Gimbutas. Others, too, view the transition as more gradual and note how the Sumerian, Egyptian, Aztec, and Inca cultures all changed from within.

More importantly, from my perspective at least, some of us are not comfortable with Gimbutas's continual references to a primordial Mother Goddess with a capital M and G. We believe this just doesn't reflect the complexity or the diversity of Neolithic religion—and feel that the complex abstract theology she attributes to the Neolithic period reflects *our way* of putting things more than it can theirs. I have even suspected that unifying prehistory under the authority of a single maternal figure may reflect our twentieth or twenty-first century longing for an undifferentiated stage of existence, for primal bliss. I would also question whether the goddesses were ever seen in such completely beneficent ways—whether the Neolithic recognition of our dependence on the natural world did not include fear as well as gratitude. And I wonder whether speaking of *the* goddess rather than the many different goddesses reflects a longing to have One Goddess of equal importance to the ONE GOD? If it reflects a view that monotheism is better? and original? And if this is a capitulation to a valorizing of the singular and abstract that some feminists have described as a "masculine" prejudice?

Greek Goddesses

At the time when interest in the goddesses first emerged as part of the so-called "second wave of feminism," some few of us, mostly Carol Christ and I, found ourselves drawn not to the Neolithic goddess (or goddesses) but rather to the goddesses of Greece. When we taught a weekend course on Goddesses in Santa Cruz early on, perhaps in 1976, what brought us together was this shared love. By now, not surprisingly, we've come to see how even our perspectives are different—though to us still complementary.

Carol, like Jane Ellen Harrison, has always been drawn primarily to the preliterary, preHomeric period of Greek civilization and to ritual and place. It isn't stories that most move her. Rather her imagination and devotion are most powerfully inspired by images, particularly by statues, by figurines small enough to hold in one's hands. By places, by excavated temple sites, and even more by the caves where worship took place long before any temples were built. By rituals through which one gets access to the life-affirming, women-empowering energy of the goddesses. Thus she has shared her commitment to a goddess-centered thealogy, not only by writing about it but by leading pilgrimages to the ancient places of goddess worship, thereby helping others enter into those places in Greece or Crete and in themselves where the goddess's presence and power and love are manifest. Carol is emphatic that to her the goddess is NOT "all that is," life & death, love & cruelty, not a-moral but intelligent, embodied love with limited power. "Her power is a limited power but she is always offering us love and hope."[7] I am deeply moved by Carol's vision of love at the heart of the universe—though I cannot share it. I have come to see—and she admits this—that her version of Goddess religion has a quasi-Christian flavor—whereas mine may be more Hebraic, more convinced that the goddesses are/were often cruel, capricious, violent.

But what I'm mostly aware of is how central myths, stories, and thus texts, are to my religious imagination—how it's my love of the differentiated goddesses with names and stories, the goddesses of literature and thus the goddesses whom we inevitably initially meet primarily as men have represented them. It's this literature that sets me imagining what these figures, these stories, might have meant to women, and how the goddesses might have been envisioned in earlier, less male-centered periods.

This focus is certainly clearly evident in *The Goddess*, which is still my favorite among the books I've written—though I am very aware I couldn't write this book now. Partly because I just know more now than I did then. Partly because I may be in a more private place. That book grew out of the only time in my life when I was living essentially alone, unpartnered. It was a time when I may have felt more free to talk about MY life without also talking about another's. But maybe just because I've done THAT. Maybe because as a Crone my interests are different. Maybe because it's a different time, the beginning of a new millennium—even though I don't know fully what that might mean.

Last year in this lecture I spoke of Freud and began by noting how he's been spoken of as the dominant intellectual presence of the century that has just ended. Perhaps the 20th century WAS his century, the century of psychoanalysis, the century of Oedipus (as the 19th century had been the century of Antigone). Perhaps this will be the century of Athene…. (I'll say a little more about this possibility further on.)

Revisioning the Goddesses

Recently I have been thinking anew of a lecture on the Oedipus myth I heard James Hillman give eight or so years ago, a lecture which didn't really sink in then. Hillman presented it at a conference on family therapy in Santa Barbara. I was scheduled to be one of the respondents. Looking around I could see how completely bewildered by the talk most of the family therapists in the room were and so most of my attention was focused on what I might say when Hillman was done that might speak to them. But in rereading I've been free to attend to what this essay says to ME. Hillman's thesis is that the Oedipus myth has indeed been the myth of the century inaugurated by Freud—not so much because we've been so focused in looking AT that myth, at the Oedipus story, but because we seem to be stuck in looking THROUGH it, that is, caught in looking at myths as a way toward SELF-UNDERSTANDING. Hillman communicates his deep respect for Freud's relocation of the human world, including the familial world, in the mythical imagination. Freud, he says, helped us to see that the actual family IS mythical. But Hillman wants us to see that Freud's Oedipus is not Sophocles'. For Sophocles the *polis* is central. What sets the play in motion is the desperate need to find a cure for the plague that is devastating the city. Finding the truth about oneself is not enough. Hillman calls for a more polytheistic view, one not dominated by this ONE myth, yet he realizes how difficult it is to get out of this myth. Even when we try to focus on a different myth, try to imagine therapy differently, through Eros and Psyche or Dionysos, or Persephone, we seem to "still be trying to find ourselves, our true story, our identity?"[8] As long as our method remains "search for self," we are caught in the Oedipus myth.

I have come to realize how true this is of my *Goddess* book. No matter what myth or mythical figure I was focusing on, I WAS looking at the myths as a way toward self-understanding. I also realize how Hillman's critique recapitulates Buber's critique of aiming at the self—and how I seem to need to learn the same lesson over and over: the right balancing for me of what I've learned from Jung and from Buber, of I and Thou. I am NOT saying there was anything wrong about what I did then when I wrote the book. I still see it as valid, as almost necessary for me then. And I'm aware of how much it still speaks to others. Nor am I saying that others will necessarily find themselves at the place in which I now find myself.

But for me that twenty-five year old dream, which keeps meaning more and more as the years go on, is now about searching for *her*, for another—more clearly than it was then. Last week a student asked me if the HER in the dream wasn't really myself in the Jungian sense of my Self. My answer—my usual answer to most questions—was "Yes and No—but definitely in a sense Yes." I had turned to the Greek goddesses (and later to the Greek gods) to help me/us see who we are and what we might become out of a deep conviction that psyche needs images to nurture its growth and that reflection on our own lives can deepen our understanding of the myths.

When I wrote *The Goddess* the classicists I was most drawn to were Carl Kerenyi and Walter Otto. Like them I was trying to capture what Kerenyi speaks of as "the essence of what the Greeks meant by Hermes" or Aphrodite or Hera, the archetypal aspect of these divinities, the psychological aspect. This meant adopting an ahistorical, achronological view, bringing together what I could learn of the preliterate understanding with all the literary evidences from Homer to Ovid and creating a kind of composite view. I was hoping in my own more awkward way to imitate Kerenyi's deceptive, graceful moving back and forth among all the strata as though all existed at once, spatially rather than temporally. It was then not a big step to see how these goddesses STILL existed, to discover their immediate contemporary psychological relevance.

I can still feel the tug of this essentialist approach. But now, as I've said, it's a different aspect of the goddesses that I find most compelling. I am less interested in how they illumine my self-understanding, more interested in the *otherness* of the Greek perspective, how it might provide *disorientation* rather than orientation. I want to find a way of honoring the historical distance, as Buber tried to honor the foreignness of the Biblical perspective in his *Verdeutsch-ing* of the Hebrew Bible.

When *The Goddess* first appeared, the criticism that most struck home was one that appeared in some classics journal to the effect that I'd ignored how for the Greeks their gods and goddesses primarily served a political function and that my psychological interpretation was anachronistic and narcissistic. I heard that and knew both that it was true and at the time irrelevant, that I'd been drawn to the goddesses because of a need to understand my woman self in all its complexity and ambiguity. Indeed, that they had drawn me to them, one by one; that my interpretation was appropriate to where I was then, and to where feminism was then at a time when it seemed to me we needed a depth psychological understanding of the feminine to balance the narrowly literal political agenda of many prominent feminists.

Nevertheless, I couldn't just brush this criticism aside. There was a way its author was right AND I was right. And I find myself now wanting, needing, to attend to this political function more explicitly, more fully, than I did then. Not as an "instead" but as an "and also." I find myself still finding that goddesses (and gods) are good to think with—but wanting to think with them, through them, about our responsibility toward the human community.

I am so much more aware now of how in cult one never simply addressed an Olympian god or goddess—but always a particular aspect or localized epiphany. A primary reason to consult an oracle was the need to discover which name or epithet one would need to use. I am also more aware that for the Greeks it was the pantheon not the gods in isolation that made visible the ordering pattern through which they imagined the natural world, the psyche, and especially human society. I have come to be more interested in looking at myths as the locus of ideological struggle, to be more drawn to the post-structuralist approach of classicists such as Jean Pierre Vernant, Nicole Loraux, Froma Zeitlin. Thus I have come to recognize that my critic was right: that for the Greeks—at least those of classical Athens—the goddesses were more important in relation to *polis* than to psyche—and that this is the aspect which now interests me.[9]

I want now to learn what I can from Nicole Loraux and others about reading myths in their civic framework. I've been especially impressed by Loraux's book *The Children of Athena: Athenian Ideas About Citizenship and the Division Between the Sexes.* She has helped give me a sense of what would be involved in looking at myths, looking at the Greek myths about the goddesses, in terms of how they are actively functioning in history, looking at how a myth was used in the city in a particular period. She makes it so evident that one can't separate myth from the city, can't look at the history of the city apart from the myths. Her focus is on the city's self-image, how it sees itself in fantasy. This, of course, includes idealization and wish-fulfillment; it involves recognizing the political efficacy of fantasy.

Loraux makes plain that she has no interest in the origins of the myths nor in their psychological relevance, only in what fifth century texts and rituals and art tell us about how myth was functioning then and there. I can't follow her in this; I want it ALL: the pre-history of the myths before their fifth century appropriation and their post-history, the psychological relevance as well as the historical function, but I DO want to "get" THIS part. For to read, as Loraux does, myths in their civic framework, to explore how they are actively functioning in history, how mythic themes mold and legitimate civic experience and get reworked seems particularly helpful when we're trying to understand the relevance of myth to political life.

Turning Again to Athene

So I want to follow Loraux's lead in turning to Athene. In Greek religion, in cult, Athene was more important than even Zeus precisely because of her association with history, human community, civilization. She was the protectress, the rescuer from every danger. The rituals performed in her temples were thought to guarantee the continued existence of a city. She WAS the community, it was through the mediation of her presence, through the wholeness-creating power of her cult, that her worshippers knew themselves as fellow-citizens. Athene keeps us in the world of others, helps us to remember the sacred importance of its problems.

But actually what I want to do, again following Loraux, is to turn not so much to Athene as to Athene and Aphrodite. I want to follow up on a line in Loraux's chapter on the *Lysistrata* in which she says "to use Athena in the service of Aphrodite and Aphrodite in the service of Athena is a feminine way of serving the city." That is, I'd like to explore how our understanding of serving the city might be deepened by looking at it through the mythic and cultic associations between these two goddesses.

It is immediately easy to recognize the tension between Athene, the virgin daughter of Zeus who seems so very male-identified, and Aphrodite, the goddess of desire and pleasure, of female beauty and sexuality; to see them as representing incommensurable perspectives. And yet we should remember the myth that relates how Athene rather than Poseidon became the patron divinity of Athens. It was the women (who in that mythic time were in the majority) who voted for Athene, and then to appease Poseidon the men promptly deprived them of their power, excluded them from citizenship. So Athene, too, is a goddess of women. And Athene makes room for Aphrodite in her own citadel; on the western slope of the Acropolis there was a shrine of Aphrodite and Eros, and near the Propylaea a shrine to Aphrodite Pandemos and Peitho (Persuasion). It's probably important also to recall that (*contra* Plato) Aphrodite Pandemos is Aphrodite as the goddess who embraces the whole people, makes available the fellow feeling, the empathy, necessary for the existence of a community.

Furthermore, the two goddesses are brought together in the *Arrephoria*, a major ritual which initiates the month long series of summer festivals which culminate in the Panathenaea, the birthday festival of the city. The Arrephoria involves two young girls, between the ages of seven and eleven, who have spent a whole year in the precincts of Athene on the Acropolis. At the end of that year in the dark of the night they are directed to carry a basket whose contents they are forbidden to discover through a hidden underground chamber to the shrine of Aphrodite in the Gardens, the shrine of Aphrodite and Eros. Then before dawn they are to bring something else back, again something secret and sacred. Though we don't know just what this ritual was understood to mean, it was obviously a female initiation ritual under the tutelage of Athene into those mysteries of female sexual identity associated with Aphrodite. The well-being of the entire city somehow was understood to depend on the right carrying out of this ritual.

Further testimony to the importance of the connection between Athene and Aphrodite in fifth century Athens is provided by the dramatists, most explicitly in Aristophanes' comedy, the *Lysistrata*. This play was written in 412 *BCE*, during the darkest period of the Peloponnesian War, a war which set Greek against Greek in a protest against Athenian imperialism and oppression. The war had begun in 431; in 404 Athens was decisively defeated. This play by Aristophanes expresses his desperate hope that some resolution might still be possible. He tried to use myth as a way of going deeper, of moving against both nationalistic fervor and despair.

The play imagines that Lysistrata, head-priestess of Athena, talks the women of Greece (not just of Athens) into seizing the Acropolis and going on a sex strike—in the hope that this will persuade their husbands to end the war and make peace. The women are for Greece rather than for identifying with the narrow literal self-interest of the individual cities from which they come. Their identification as women, with other women, takes precedence over their political loyalties. Yet what they do they do for the sake of men as well as women, and for their own city.

The women, of course, complain about the difficulty of leaving their households, but Lysistrata persuades them this duty is more important than their ordinary domestic duties: "The hope of all the states rests on us." She tells them that their recognition of how much they would miss their men (and sex) is exactly what shows that this is the only way to get the men to make peace, for the men will miss them just as much.

"We must abstain from the joys of love," she tells them.
"Never, let the war go on," they reply at first
"What if our husbands leave us?" they ask.
"We'll find some substitute." she responds.

And so the women swear to abstain from love and love's delights, to sleep as vestals alone at nights—but they swear by Aphrodite and call upon her to make them irresistibly attractive to the men they plan to repulse. They agree to act in accord with their reputations, to inflame men's desires, to use all their seductive wiles—but to do so for the sake of the city and of all Greece. They leave their marriage beds—but in order to return their husbands to them.

They occupy the Acropolis precisely because it belongs to *Athena Parthenos,* Virginal Athene, because it is a place where they can't succumb to desire without impiety. There, they, too, under Athena's protection, will be virgins. They have in a sense returned—temporarily—to their childhood years when they had participated in civic service to the virgin goddess—who secretly sent them to Aphrodite.

They may feel desire but they have sworn to Aphrodite to serve her by not yielding to her power, though they find this difficult. There's a wonderful scene of husband-sick women trying to leave the citadel. One complains that Athene's serpent frightens her; another that Athena's owl keeps her awake. Several claim they need to go home to protect their woolens against moths or to spin their unspun flax. One claims to be starting labor, but Lysistrata finds she has hidden the helmet from the statue of *Athena Promachus,* Warrior Athene, under her skirt to feign a belly swollen with child.

Of course, at first the men dismiss "this silly disturbance." "Fools," the Magistrate berates the women, "What on earth can possess you to meddle with matters of war and matters of peace?" The impassioned (and hilarious) exchange between him and Lysistrata begins with her mocking parody, "War is the care and business of men," and ends when the chorus of women has dressed him up as a spinning-woman with her triumphant affirmation, "War is the care and business of women."

One of the women pretends to be unable to stay away from her husband. She comes to him and says she can't wait to have sex with him, but then says it just won't work unless they have first a pallet, then a mattress, then a pillow, a rug, some special ointment. He gets more and more turned on; indeed, he gets a permanent erection—and then she leaves him. "You'll vote for peace," she calls as she scampers back up to the summit of the Acropolis.

As, of course, he does—as do the other men as well.

The women triumph and so does Aphrodite, as the joint men's and women's choruses' song in her praise makes clear—but so does Athens and thus Athena.

Aristophanes' myth is of course only an illusion—mostly, I believe, a cry of pain over what won't happen, can't happen, except on the stage—and yet it suggests that to be able to imagine such a resolution, nonetheless, means something, is itself a gift. His play reminds us that as we try to understand our relation to the communal world, our life together, we need to honor both Athena and Aphrodite.

I see Aristophanes' play as reminding us of the importance of caring about the people involved, all of them, in any political struggle. For Lysistrata and those who joined her this meant caring about not just the women, not just the citizens of their own state. We can easily transpose this into the political situations in which we find ourselves. The play reminds us of the importance of trying to move beyond our own perspective and trying to imagine that of the others involved. This, I believe, is at the heart of that "imagining the real" which Martin Buber spoke of. Buber used the phrase to turn our attention to the central role the imagination plays in that empathic turning to the other which lies at the heart of any genuine communion between one human being and another and thus at the heart of human community.

I see Aristophanes' play as also reminding us of the importance of remembering that the political arena is a sacred realm—what happens there matters, really matters—and what happens there depends on us, though we may need to invoke the goddesses for help. Of course I know this is not as simple as it sounds. And so I want to end today with the same quotation with which I began *The Goddess* those many years ago. It comes from James Hillman, who reminds us:

Myths can't tell us how, they simply give us the invisible background which starts us imagining, questioning, going deeper.[10]

Notes

1.   Starhawk, "Marija Gimbutas' Work and the Question of the Sacred," in Joan Marler, ed., *From the Realm of the Ancestors: An Anthology in Honor of Marija Gimbutas* (Manchester, CT: Knowledge, Ideas & Trends, Inc., 1997) 522.

2.   Quoted in the introduction to Marler, *Realm*, 3.

3.   Marija Gimbutas, *The Gods and Goddesses of Old Europe* (Berkeley and Los Angeles: University of California Press, 1982) 197.

4. Marija Gimbutas, *The Language of the Goddess* (San Francisco: Harper & Row, 1989) 321.

5. Naomi Goldenberg, "Marija Gimbutas and the King's Archaeologist," in Marler, *Realm*, 42.

6. Cf. Mary Zeiss Stange, *Woman the Hunter* (Boston: Beacon Press, 1997).

7. Carol Christ, *Rebirth of the Goddess* (Reading, MA: Addison-Wesley, 1997).

8. James Hillman, "Oedipus Revisited," in Karl Kerenyi and James Hillman, *Oedipus Variations* (Dallas: Spring Publications, 1991) 142.

9. Once again I discover that this redirection is not mine alone. I have just been reading Bruce Lincoln's *Theorizing Myth* in which he writes of his turn away from the perspectives of a dearly loved teacher, Mircea Eliade, from Eliade's focus on the polarities of sacred and profane, cosmos and history, his focus on ecstatic experience as being the central themes of myth. Now he says, he would define myth as "ideology through narrative" and now sees as of primary importance the role myths play in political power struggles.

10. James Hillman, *ReVisioning Psychology* (New York: Harper & Row, 1975) 158.

7

Meetings and Mismeetings: A Return to Martin Buber

My decision to focus on Martin Buber in this year's Christine Downing Lecture grew out of remembering that in an important sense it is because of Buber that I first came to San Diego State.

I had written my dissertation on him and during the early years of working on it had approached Maurice Friedman for help in finding some untranslated materials he had cited in his seminal book on Buber which I'd not been able to locate. Maury responded warmly and generously, seemed genuinely interested in the particular approach to Buber that was my focus, and indicated an openness to further consultations. In a way that I had not expected that initial meeting led into an important friendship.

I was even given an opportunity to reciprocate a little for all the help Maury had given me when some years later he asked me if I'd be willing to read the manuscript of the first volume of his Buber biography. The publisher had asked for deep cuts and of course it hurt Maury to even think of leaving out any of the material he had put such effort into locating, integrating, organizing. Not surprisingly he was rather appalled by how vigorously I wrote "cut," "omit", "shorten" all over his manuscript and yet remarkably appreciative as well.

Then in 1974 when I decided it was time for me to take a sabbatical from my teaching position at Rutgers and from my marriage and wanted to do so dramatically by spending the year in California, I wrote to everyone I knew asking for help. Maury who'd moved to SDSU a year earlier replied and suggested I apply to fill in for Allan Anderson who was planning a sabbatical leave.

I applied.
I was invited to come.
I came.

And stayed.

And, of course, immediately realized I was not going to be teaching Buber here, not with Maury Friedman as a colleague!

So I never did do much in my almost 20 years of teaching here to honor explicitly my debts to Buber—though, yes, I'd include some discussion of the misunderstandings between Buber and Jung when I taught my semester long class on Jung, and said a little about Buber in my classes on Religion and Psychology or on Contemporary Theology, but that was about it. And during those years I didn't return to reread Buber either or to reflect consciously on his continuing importance to me.

But I've become aware now of it's being time to do that: to reflect on that importance, to honor it, to honor the way in which what I learned from Buber remains central to my way of being in the world, to honor how his themes have taken up residence in my soul.

A few years ago in speaking of Freud in this lecture series I said that I see Freud as the father of my soul, as I see Jung as my soul's mother. Today I want to put it differently, want to say that I see both Freud and Buber as my Jewish grandfathers (both versions are of course true).

My actual grandfather (who stayed in Germany when my own family left and whom I never saw again after I was four) was Jewish but not really. He'd, for purely practical reasons, become an Anglican as a young man, married a Viennese Catholic, raised his children as Lutheran. He never really filled that Jewish grandfather place in my soul, as Buber and Freud—whom I discovered in my mid to late 20s—have.

I've often said that the way I understand Freud stems from my having come to him from Jung—so that I read him poetically, metaphorically, mythically. But I should say just as emphatically that the way I understand Freud grows out of my coming to him from Buber—so that I read him in a way that emphasizes his recognition of the interpenetration of self and others, his understanding of how our very selves are constructed through our interactions with others, and his conviction of the importance of our being able to make the move from narcissism to eros.

So today I want to talk about *this* grandfather—and want to do so by exploring the theme, Meetings and Mismeetings. I want to talk about what I've learned from Buber about the importance of those moments in our lives where we are fully present to and with another and about the retrospective importance of those moments when we come to realize we were not.

Perhaps a way of beginning to communicate what I most want to about Buber is to speak of the autobiography he wrote toward the end of his life, his *Meetings,* and to note what in retrospect, as a man in his 80s, he sees as the most significant moments in his life. As the title suggests, for Buber it is meetings with actual human others—friends and strangers, literally present others but also others present through their creations—Bach and the Baal Shem Tov, Kant and Nietzsche—and nonhuman others: a tree, a cat, a horse. Meetings where we've felt ourselves in the presence of the sacred, the transformative. Meetings with another whose simple being there toward us has made us fully present to them. Meetings which have seemed to include not just ourselves and another, but a third presence, the spirit, the between itself, which makes possible a full presentness that usually eludes us.

Martin Buber has himself been one of those by whom I've been met in this way—even though I never met him personally, only through his books and (just to complicate things) in my dreams.

I want to share those dreams with you—but before that I want to include an account by Buber of a series of his own dreams, an account with which he opens his 1929 book, *Between Man and Man.* He entitled these few pages "Original Remembrance."[1]

> Through all sorts of changes the same dream, sometimes after an interval of several years, recurs to me. I name it the dream of the double cry. Its context is always much the same, a "primitive" world meagrely equipped. I find myself in a vast cave, like the Latomias of Syracuse, or in a mud building that reminds me when I awake of the villages of the *fellahin,* or on the fringe of a gigantic forest whose like I cannot remember having seen.
>
> The dream begins in very different ways, but always with something extraordinary happening to me, for instance, with a small animal resembling a lion-cub (whose name I know in the dream but not when I awake) tearing the flesh from my arm and being forced only with an effort to loose its hold. The strange thing is that this first part of the dream story, which in the duration as well as the outer meaning of the incidents is easily the most important, always unrolls at a furious pace as though it did not matter. Then suddenly the pace abates: I stand there and cry out. In the view of the events which my waking consciousness has I should have to suppose that the cry I utter varies in accordance with what preceded it, and is sometimes joyous, sometimes fearful, sometimes even filled both with pain and with triumph. But in my morning recollection it is neither so expressive nor so various. Each time it is the same cry, inarticulate but in strict rhythm, rising and falling, swelling to a fulness which my throat could not endure were I awake, long and slow, quiet, quite slow and very long, a cry that is a song. When it ends my heart stops beating.

But then, somewhere, far away, another cry moves towards me, another which is the same, the same cry uttered or sung by another voice. Yet it is not the same cry, certainly no "echo" of my cry but rather its true rejoinder, tone for tone not repeating mine, not even in a weakened form, but corresponding to mine, answering its tones—so much so, that mine, which at first had to my own ear no sound of questioning at all, now appear as questions, as a long series of questions, which now all receive a response. The response is no more capable of interpretation than the question. And yet the cries that meet the one cry that is the same do not seem to be the same as one another. Each time the voice is new. But now, as the reply ends, in the first moment after its dying fall, a certitude, true dream certitude comes to me that *now it has happened*. Nothing more. Just this, and in this way—*now it has happened*. If I should try to explain it, it means that that happening which gave rise to my cry has only now, with the rejoinder, really and undoubtedly happened.

After this manner the dream has recurred each time—till once, the last time, now two years ago. At first it was as usual (it was the dream with the animal) my cry died away, again my heart stood still. But then there was quiet. There came no answering call. I listened, I heard no sound. For I *awaited* the response for the first time; hitherto it had always surprised me, as though I had never heard it before. Awaited, it failed to come. But now something happened with me. As though I had till now had no other access from the world to sensation save that of the ear and now discovered myself as a being simply equipped with senses, both those clothed in the bodily organs and the naked senses, so I exposed myself to the distance, open to all sensation and perception. And then, not from a distance but from the air round about me, noiselessly, came the answer. Really it did not come; it was there. It had been there—so I may explain it—even before my cry: there it was, and now, when I laid myself open to it, it let itself be received by me. I received it as completely into my perception as ever I received the rejoinder in one of the earlier dreams. If I were to report with what I heard it I should have to say "with every pore of my body." As ever the rejoinder came in one of the earlier dreams this corresponded to and answered my cry. It exceeded the earlier rejoinder in an unknown perfection which is hard to define, for it resides in the fact that it was already there. When I had reached an end of receiving it, I felt again that certainty, pealing out more than ever, that *now it has happened*.

Alongside this dream of Buber's I'd like to lay two of my own.

The first is a dream I dreamt when I was in my midtwenties, almost forty-five years ago. I was expecting my fourth child. I had just recently discovered Jung. This was one of the first dreams I recorded after being reminded by Jung how important our dreams can be.

In this dream I found myself bicycling through a woods like those conjured up when my mother read to me from the Household Tales collected by the Brothers Grimm, like the woods in the tale of Hansel and Gretel or of Little Red Ridinghood. Because the path I had to take was an unfamiliar one I held in my right hand, which also gripped the steering bar, a handdrawn map. The path was a narrow dirt one, with deeply marked ruts and barely concealed rocks, frequently crisscrossed by protruding roots. There were many forks.

Once as I took my eyes from the road to check my map, the bicycle hit an especially large root. I lost my balance and fell off the bike. The map flew out of my hand and back behind me. After I'd picked myself up, dusted off my hands and clothes, and righted my bicycle, I knew I needed to recover the map before I could proceed along my way. So I turned around and began on foot to retrace my way, looking along the path and its periphery.

I walked quite a distance without success and then saw, just a little further on, a figure sitting across the path with his back against a tree who held something in his hand and who seemed to be beckoning me to approach. As I came nearer I saw he was a whitebearded, wizened old man with deepset eyes and a friendly countenance. But what he wordlessly put in my hands when I reached him was not my map but a living clump of grass.

The dream ended there. Its impact did not. I felt the dream had showed me how much until then I had relied on maps, plans, predrawn schemas to guide me through my life. After the dream I began to trust to a more spontaneous, more organic, more growing-from-within kind of guidance. Though it may sound romantic, I felt the dream had changed my life. Among other things it prepared me to welcome my fifth (unplanned) pregnancy as a gift—and somehow it didn't seem surprising at all that this child should be my first daughter!

A few years later a friend and I were talking about Jung and my sense of how much I'd learned from him but how much I now needed a new teacher, one who would understand better than Jung seemed to how the sacred comes to us in our meetings with one another and not only in our engagements with our own deepest selves. He suggested I read Martin Buber. I resisted. Others, earlier, had urged *I and Thou* on me. I'd respected their sense of what might speak to me, had read the first few pages, and then each time put the book aside.

This friend insisted. He put in my hands his own wellworn copy of *Between Man and Man*. I turned the book over and there on the back cover was the face of the wise old man of my dream. I took the book. I read it. I ended up writing my dissertation on Buber.

Some ten years after I'd finished that dissertation, by now a good twenty since I'd had the dream, during my first spring in California, now more than twenty-five years ago, I had another dream.

This time I was in the desert not in a woods. I'd come there because I knew I was lost, dispirited and directionless. I'd started out at twilight from the city and driven far into the night, along increasingly unfamiliar and narrow roads. Then one of my tires had gone flat and I'd discovered I had no spare.

In the distance I saw a flickering light which I thought might come from a house whence I might telephone for help. I started walking in its direction but gradually realized that I seemed to be getting no closer and that I was less sure now that there was a light at all. It seemed obvious that it would be best after all simply to return to my car and wait for the help that would surely eventually appear. But when I turned around I discovered there was no car. Indeed, even the road had disappeared. Now I was truly lost. I had no idea what to do next.

And then suddenly from behind a large sagebush there appeared a bent and wrinkled, kindly looking old man. This time I recognized him. It was Martin Buber again. "Can I help you?" he asked. "No," I replied. "You and I have been through this before. It is time now for me to go in search of Her."

And thus began the involvement with Greek goddesses, with feminist theology, with the psychology of women, that has occupied me for the last twenty-five years and more.

But I find it intriguing that Buber reappeared as a guide at that moment. In the dream once he addressed me, I seemed to know exactly how to proceed. I made my way directly through the still unfamiliar, still untracked desert to the cave deep under the earth where She awaited me.

I hadn't thought about it in that way until a few years ago. I'd always thought of my turning to the goddesses as a turning away from earlier perspectives. But now I recognize how much continuity there has been, the kind of continuity represented by the living clump of grass, not by any map I could have drawn beforehand.

As I reflect now on what led me to put myself under Buber's tutelage during the many years it takes to complete a dissertation, I see how much it was because of his articulation of perspectives which seemed more congruent with my own than was true of any of the other theologians whose work I'd studied. I found Buber saying things I knew, but hadn't quite known I knew, hadn't had words for. He offered me a way to be followed because it lay along my own beginning way. I didn't then think of this in terms of feminist perspectives or women's ways of looking at things, although now I would.

I think I responded to *Between Man and Man* as I hadn't at first to *I and Thou* because in the later book Buber communicates more directly that he is speaking on the basis of concrete personal experiences which require him to speak. As he does also in *Meetings*.

I felt him opening me to aspects of my own experience which I had hitherto ignored. I felt that I was meant as he spoke, that he intended me—not as when I read Jung that I was listening in on a monologue by someone some of whose experiences remarkably paralleled my own nor as when I read some philosophers whose works had deeply impressed me that I was meant because all are meant. I felt addressed in all my particularity, understood, in part, but, even more significantly, challenged, called.

I was then able to read *I and Thou* and respond to its spiralling lyricism. I could now hear the I and the Thou in a different way—as *Ich* and *Du*. I could hear the sounding of the familiar *du*, the "you" by which I (born in Germany) had been addressed as a child and not the formal, archaic "Thou" which had left me unmoved.

I am struck here—as I also am when I think of how badly served Freud has been by his translators—by how radically translation can be betrayal. Freud's *Seele*, the German word for "soul" is so radically misrepresented when rendered as "mental structure," his *Ich,* the everyday word for "I," so different in its connotations from "ego." I have come to see how truly difficult it is to render Buber's *Ich* and his *Du,* and thus his central insights in another language.

For *Du* IS more than our everyday "you." It is the most intimate form of address imaginable—and in this sense there is something sacred about it, which Ronald Gregor Smith tried to communicate by rendering it as "Thou." The specialness of this *Du* was more true for my parents' generation than for mine and especially more than it is for Germans born after World War II—but it was even more true in Buber's time when it often took years before friends agreed to use it with one another.

I think in this connection of an encounter recorded in the Prelude to Buber's *Eclipse of God.*[2] He writes there of a man who asked him "How can you still use the word 'God'? What word of human speech is so misused, so defiled, so desecrated. All the innocent blood that has been shed for it has robbed it of its radiance."

Buber answered: "Yes, indeed, it is the most heavy-laden of all human words. None has become so soiled, so mutilated. Just for this reason I may not abandon it. Generations of men have laid the burden of their anxious lives upon this word and weighed it to the ground; it lies in the dust and bears their whole burden…We cannot cleanse the word God and we cannot make it whole; but, defiled and mutilated as it is, we can raise it from the ground and set it over an hour of great care."

When Buber stopped speaking, the old man came over, put his hand on Buber's shoulder, and said: "Let us say *Du* to one another."

Can you hear how this *Du* communicates the sacredness of real intimacy? feel the inner meaning of a formality we may at first be inclined to regard as anachronistic?

I value so much how Buber communicates that his speaking always takes place "on the way," at a particular point along his way; how he communicates that he is speaking from a particular place in his own life, and speaking in relation to a particular other, at a particular historical time.

I value even more that he reveals that some of what he knows he knows because of failures and limitations. There's a significant sense, I believe, in which *Meetings* should really be called *Meetings and Mismeetings*. For it's as though Buber learns that all real life is meeting from the many times when the meeting doesn't happen.

After reading *Between Man And Man* I could also hear Buber's "I" differently, could hear in his *Ich* the voice that arose from a failed encounter with a young man who had come to see him on the eve of World War I. This is an important moment; in *Between Man And Man* Buber called it "A Conversion;"[3] later he called it "A Conversation." The meeting, he says, was perfectly friendly, but he had not been there "in spirit," had not been attentive enough to guess the questions which his visitor did not put.

> What do we expect when we are in despair and yet go to a man? Surely a presence by means of which we are told that nevertheless there is meaning. "Since then I have given up the 'religious' which is nothing but the exception, exaltation, ecstasy. I possess nothing but the everyday out of which I am never taken…If that is religion then it is just everything, all that is lived in its possibility of dialogue."

I think of other failed meetings Buber recounts, for instance, the mismeeting with the worker whose secure agnostic *Weltanshauung* Buber shattered. "I do not need God to feel at home in the world," the young man claims in a discussion after a lecture. Buber initially responds by overwhelming the uneducated young man with philosophical arguments and is then dismayed as the man says "You are right."[4]

Most powerfully, in Buber's *Ich* I also now hear the voice of the child whose mother had left him without bidding him farewell, the child who learned from a neighbor child, "She will never come back."[5] "I suspect that all I have learned about genuine meeting during my life had its first origin in that hour on the balcony," Buber wrote. Eventually he comes to recognize the archetypal aspect of that separation: "I began to perceive it as something that concerned all men not just me."

This recognition of how the primal separation from the mother—which we all experience—issues in a lifelong longing for connection, for being fully affirmed, fully met (the same recognition I believe which for Freud came as the discovery "I am Oedipus!")—is indeed at the heart of Buber's understanding of our human being-here.

What most moves me in Buber—I see this as at the center of his gift to all of us—is his affirmation of the sacredness of those moments when we are really there with another, as though it were those moments that life was really for, as though it is those moments in which we most truly experience the presence of the divine.

As one of the many who can no longer say *Du* to the 'dead' known God, I bless Buber's saying that everything depends on whether we can still say it to the living unknown God by saying "du" with all our being to another living and known person. This stirs me because it accords so deeply with my own experience—as does Buber's affirmation that such meetings happen in the most ordinary, everyday contexts, not only in moments of high drama, in the "volcanic hours."

I value Buber's recognition of the primary word "I-you" and understood why to begin with it needed to be distinguished from the other primary word, "I-it;" but I value even more his recognition of how inevitably intermingled these words, these worlds, are.

I value Buber's growing clarity as to how different encounter is from mystical fusion, communion from union, the everyday from ecstasy. At the time he wrote *I and Thou*, I believe he still had trouble clearly distinguishing the primal closeness of the bond between mother and infant from communion, meeting, dialogue, though he did see how the separation from the primal bond with the mother issues in yearning—not for a literal incestual return to her as some claim Freud believed or for a renewed contact with one's own inner depths as Jung suggested—but rather in a yearning for a "you," a yearning to be fully met by another.

I think many of us have trouble learning how to say "you" in a way that really respects the otherness of the other and of ourselves, a you-saying predicated on distance and relation, on separation and attachment, a you-saying which is also an I-saying but not the I-saying of the fully autonomous, wholly independent I of I-it.

Buber sometimes says, "Only an I can say you." At other times he tells us, "I become I as I say you." Both are true. Neither alone quite is.

And I'd add, as Buber came to, "I become I as 'you' is said to me." In his later works Buber honors the centrality of our longing for confirmation, confirmation of who I am and of who I can become. "I secretly and bashfully wish for a 'yes,' which allows me to be," he says.

Buber also recognizes how difficult it is for us to show ourselves as we really are. Among the most powerful passages for me when I first read *Between Man and Man* was the one in which Buber spoke of how readily we can fall into "seeming," how readily substitute the pretense of dialogue for an actual reaching out to the other. I felt he knew this because he'd learned it in his own life. I remember still how powerfully this passage struck me when I read it as a young woman: how I felt seen in both a judging and a creatively challenged way, and forced to recognize how much I fled from risking true encounter, from the really being seen that I most deeply coveted.

We want real connection so badly, but most of us are early on wounded in this capacity, so we hide behind a persona, behind "seeming," out of our deep longing to be found lovable. But, of course, love for the mask doesn't really assuage the yearning. Buber believes that we all begin as open to others, but that early experiences of being rejected or abandoned may lead us to grow defenses so that the capacity for true meeting dams up and we find ourselves in flight from meeting. And yet a restlessness of the soul for genuine meeting with others remains. The search for the "you" lies hidden behind the years of self-protectiveness.

Buber describes so beautifully what real encounter is like. He speaks of a "bold swinging" into the other's life which affirms that other's ultimate mysteriousness.

> This person is other, essentially other than myself, and this otherness of his is what I mean, because I mean him; I confirm it; I wish his otherness to exist…That he does not have merely a different mind, or way of thinking or feeling, or a different conviction or attitude, but has also a different perception of the world, a different recognition and order of meaning, a different touch from the regions of existence, a different faith, a different soil: to affirm all this, to affirm it in the way of a creature, in the midst of the hard situations of conflict, without relaxing their real seriousness—that is what I mean by I and you.[6]

I have suggested several times that Buber himself only gradually came to recognize the difference between union and communion, fusion and encounter. It was a profound immersion with the Hebrew Bible that began in midlife which clarified this for him, which taught him to see the "You" spoken *to* me as more central than the "You" that I speak. He learned this from his sense of the transformative power of the "You" God addressed to Adam, Abraham, Moses, and the prophets. He thus came to believe that I can say "You" because "You" has been said to me, because I have been met as a person.

Unlike many Biblically-based theologians who find in the Bible a radical distinction between humans and the natural world, between history and nature, Buber believed that we are related to the other living beings with whom we live on this earth not as "things," as objects for our use, but as personlike, that we live with them in mutuality and reciprocity. He wrote very beautifully of the I-you relation at the "threshold of speech" which we have, not with Nature in a capital N kind of way, but with particular creatures, with the cat whose eye momentarily caught his own, with the horse whose life beneath his stroking hand he felt.

And yet I also agree with Buber about the specialness of human-human relationships where actual *words* are possible. I think in this connection of how after the most intimate sexual encounter, we want to ask, "and how was it for you?"

Buber also understands that real meeting may happen in silence, in silence that *is* communication—and that real meeting does not mean agreement. Rather it means turning with all our being to an other and knowing that this other's whole being is turned to me. It means the kind of event that issues in "Let us say *Du* to one another."

There is such a strange and subtle interplay between meetings and mismeetings. We may learn so much of how important real connection is from the sadness we feel afterwards when it didn't quite happen after all and we feel it could have. We know we *can't* always be fully present, can't possibly. We are surprised—and deeply grateful—when it happens in moments we'd never have expected it too.

But it is, I believe, what we're here for.

Like Buber I'd say: "All real living is meeting."

Notes

1. Martin Buber, *Between Man and Man* (New York: Macmillan, 1975) 1–3.

2. Martin Buber, *Eclipse of God* (New York: Harper, 1952) 6–9. The English translation has the old man say, "Let us be friends." But the German reads, "*Wir sollen uns jetzt Du sagen.*"

3. *Between*, 13–15.

4. *Eclipse*, 4–5.

5. Martin Buber, *Meetings* (La Salle, IL: Open Court, 1973) 17–19.

6. *Between*, 168.

8

Greek Tragedy in Its Historical Hour—and in Ours

Each year at Christmastime, or usually a little later, I send out one of those annual letters; it's a way of staying in touch with friends and family, many of whom I get to see only rarely, but also a way of getting in touch with myself, of looking back over a year just passed and discovering what among all that happened stands out in retrospect as truly memorable, as in significant ways defining. These annual lectures—this is already the eighth!—have come to serve a similar function for me. Each spring I have to decide: What do I most want to talk about this year? Early on each lecture seemed complete in itself, as originally the essays which ended up being chapters of my book *The Goddess* had seemed wholly independent of one another—until eventually I realized that together they represented a particular body of work, that they complemented one another, belonged together, together comprised a whole. As I'm slowly beginning to realize these lectures do as well.

Once I saw that, I began to realize there are some recurrent themes and perspectives that mark my current preoccupations, among them a deepening interest in history, in what biblical stories or Greek myths or goddess traditions can tell me about those who originally told and retold them rather than—at least immediately—in what they can tell me about myself.

Last year my lecture focused on Martin Buber, but I think I didn't talk about what is for me one of his most important papers, one called "Prophecy, Apocalyptic and the Historical Hour."[1] In this essay, written during the Second World War, Buber wrote of his sense of the importance of our recovering the prophetic conviction that what happens in history depends on *us*, not on some miraculous *deus ex machina* rescue. He sought to persuade us that we can never know the limits of the possible except by going all the way to those limits. The essay communicates Buber's deep belief in the relevance of the biblical perspective to his own historical hour.

This year I would like to do something somewhat similar, to talk about the relevance of Greek tragedy to *our* historical hour. Or rather *not* talk directly about that, to leave that for us to reflect on as I explore its relevance to its own historical hour.

I've recently become fascinated by how differently we view Greek tragedy now than when I was in school, how we bring questions to it that reflect our postmodern, post-Holocaust, post-feminist, post-9/11 sensibilities, how we see problems, conflicts, uncertainties where we used to see assurance, nobility. I was in college 50 years ago, just after World War II, at a time when what we'd learned about the Holocaust made us newly aware of the reality of human cruelty and human vulnerability and at a time when the threat of nuclear devastation seemed very immediate. Nevertheless, the dominant rhetoric about the Holocaust emphasized the themes of liberation and survivor resilience, and the Allied triumph over the Nazis seemed to provide evidence of the ultimate triumph of good over evil.

So it is perhaps not surprising that at that time we viewed Greek tragedy in terms of its representations of human courage and dignity. We saw it as expressive of a commitment to justice and truth and as testifying to the existence of an ultimately trustworthy, though often hidden, moral order. There was general agreement that of the three tragedians whose work had survived—Aeschylus, Sophocles, and Euripides—Sophocles was the deepest, the one whose perspectives were closest to our own. We viewed the Greeks as being in touch with perennial truths about human nature and the moral universe. We read their plays to discover what they might tell us about ourselves.[2] And because the then-dominant trend in literary criticism was what was called the "New Criticism," our focus was radically *intratextual*, calling for close attention to the internal structure of the literary text being examined and particularly to the way recurrent images weave the whole together.

Now we seem to look differently, to ask different questions and to adopt different interpretive strategies. For, as reception theory suggests, every generation will inevitably have its own Greeks (as it has its own Moses, its own Jesus). Where, for example, the teachers of my youth saw undiluted optimism at the end of the *Oresteia,* contemporary scholars see Aeschylus voicing a cautious hope. Our present way of looking at Greek tragedy clearly owes a great deal to our having learned from Claude Lévi-Strauss to look for the polarities and oppositions that structure any system, to look for the subsurface tensions. Now, as Bruce Lincoln says in his important book, *Theorizing Myth*, we have learned to look at myths as ideology in narrative form, and thus (to extend his observation in an obvious way) to look at tragedy as ideology in dramatic form, as ideology in contestation. For that, of course is what drama *is: agon*, struggle. It presents us with the interaction of competing ideologies, political interests, value systems.

We have come to appreciate Euripides more than we did earlier, to admire his irony, his anomalies, his flaunting of theatrical conventions, his self-reflexivity. We are especially intrigued, I believe, by his representations of women, his Medea, his Phaedra, his Hecuba. We are impressed by his ability to enter into their inner world, by his recognition of how the wrongs done to and by women are integrally related. That Euripides has been called both a misogynist and a protofeminist seems like such a perfect example of the way in which we now view tragedy as leaving things open, exploiting ambiguities, presenting rather than resolving contradictions.

We now read with more interest in social context and in *inter*-textuality, in the particular ways the tragedians rework Homer and in the ways Euripides deliberately echoes and rewrites Aeschylus and Sophocles. "The characters," Simon Goldhill notes, "carry around echoes of their textual pasts."[3] (Much has been written, for example, comparing the Orestes of the *Odyssey* with Orestes as each of the tragedians represents him.) Whereas earlier Homer was viewed merely as an inherited resource for the poets of the fifth century, it now seems evident to us that the dramatists' engagement with his texts represents an active questioning about the kind of authority the past he represents has in their own world. The dramatists seem to experience themselves as both standing in and outside of the inherited tradition.

I have come to find it intriguing that tragedy arises at a very specific period in Athenian history and that it survives as a vital genre for only the approximately 70-year period spanned by its extant examples. This leads me to wonder why: What particular social, philosophical, religious, psychological, and literary developments encourage its rise and what factors lead to its ebbing. The oldest surviving Greek tragedy, Aeschylus' *Persians,* was performed in 472 BCE, a scant eight years after the defeat of the Persians at Salamis; the last surviving tragedies, Sophocles' *Oedipus at Colonus* and Euripides' *Iphigenia at Aulis* and *Bacchae*, were all three performed posthumously in 405, just before Athens' decisive defeat in the Peloponnesian War. Obviously, this was a time of radical transition and upheaval. It was a time when the divergence between the heroic values of the archaic world and those of the relatively newly established and still fragile law-centered democracy was still painful and troubling, and when the long drawn out Peloponnesian War heightened awareness of the limitations and precariousness of the civic order. It was a time of conflict between the values of the family-based past and those of the new polis-centered world, that is, a time when the priority of political over familial commitments was still recent and tenuous. (Think of the many plays in which this conflict is central: Aeschylus' *Oresteia*, Sophocles' *Antigone*, Euripides' *Iphigenia at Aulis*, to name just one by each dramatist.) This conflict could also be expressed as a conflict between chthonic and Olympian deities, between *physis* and *nomos*, nature and culture, between women and men. Thus we now view classical Athens as a locus of tension between competing values and irresolvable polarities. The tragedies were written to illuminate—not resolve—these tensions. For that is what drama is: *agon*, struggle, the representation of multiple perspectives.

It is also relevant, I believe, to note that tragedy in Athens arises more or less concurrently with philosophy and historical writing, that is, at a time when there was a growing appreciation of the distinction between *mythos* and *logos*, between the language of storytelling and that of abstract discourse, and essentially disappears in the next century when the conflict between mythic and conceptual discourse seems to have been resolved. That is, in the fourth century the philosophers rather than the poets had come to be recognized as the masters of truth (to use Marcel Detienne's phrase). Aristotle's *Poetics* thus represents a retrospective look back at a genre whose heyday is clearly past. Jean-Pierre Vernant says that for Aristotle "tragic man" is already a stranger. Aristotle no longer really "gets" the inner tension between past and present or between fate and agency, so salient in the previous century.[4] For tragedy both explanations, external determination and personal responsibility, are simultaneously true; there is always what Freud called "over-determination." Oedipus is both a victim of fate and responsible for his deeds. Orestes is both guilty of the most heinous of all crimes, matricide, and a son dutifully avenging his father's murder. Both Antigone and Creon are right. And both are wrong!

Fifth-century Athens was full of talk, competitive and argumentative talk, persuasive and manipulative talk—in the law courts, the agora, the gymnasia, the symposia—and the theater. This is the era of the Sophists (the nominalists, empiricists, and might-makes-right philosophers against whom Socrates argued). Everything was up for debate, even the most fundamental assumptions about justice, virtue, piety. (Many of the most dramatic scenes in the tragedies resemble the arguments that might have been heard in the law courts or between rival philosophers.) Somewhat as during the Italian Renaissance, there was an exuberant sense of living in a *new* time. We cannot help but be struck by the tremendous faith in human rationality, in the ever-growing human control of the natural world, in progress. (Think of the "Ode to Man" in the *Antigone* that voices a per-spective eerily like the shallow optimism so characteristic of European thinking in the decades before the outbreak of the First World War—and not so different from some views still put forward today.) But it is also a time characterized by a new relativistic skepticism about the security of any rational position and by a recognition of how easily human confidence and assertiveness can overreach and become destructive.[5]

Fifth century Athens was also full of cultic activity. There was a communal festival scheduled on at least one-third of the days of the year. A major part of the city's budget went toward financing these celebrations and the wealthy competed with one another in contributing to the public displays. Thus, the gods were still important. Worship of them, especially of Zeus and Athene, was still a vital part of civil life. For Greek religion in the classical period cultic participation, not individual "belief in" the gods, was central. Long before Durkheim, sophisticated Athenians seem to have recognized that their shared acts of worship, their com-munal rituals, made them a community. Long before Jung, they seem to have recognized their gods and goddesses as projections of human psychology and human society, as made by us, and yet as naming permanent, archetypal energies.

In tragedy religious convictions and not only political commitments are sub-jected to radical questioning. Although the gods rarely enter the action of the plays (except for Athene and Apollo in the *Eumenides* and Dionysos in the *Bac-chae*) they are always present through the invocations of the characters and the chorus. The tragedians seem especially concerned to show how we cannot afford to ignore the chthonic deities (or the aspects of human experience they embody) not centrally important in current civic cult—especially Hades, Dionysos, Hek-ate, Eros, and Aphrodite. For Sophocles the gods are still there as forces outside us that to be human we must recognize and honor; they represent external forces that shape our destiny and challenge us to meet it with dignity and courage. For Euripides the gods are still there as forces at work in us that we ignore at our peril, forces which cannot be tamed but that must be acknowledged.

But the human relationship to the gods is more problematic in tragedy than in epic. In Homer at moments of decision a god intervenes (or one alternative emerges as clearly the more profitable). But already in Aeschylus we see Orestes standing alone between the imperatives represented by Apollo and the Furies. His struggle between them pushes him inward, makes him aware of an inner division; he cannot act with the spontaneity or certainty of a Homeric hero. Tragic protag-onists are caught struggling between two alternatives in a way that leads to a new depth of soul. Choice is unavoidable; none of the available choices is really wholly right, yet in the end the tragic hero is compelled to choose. Thus "the hero has ceased to be a model. He has become, both for himself and others, a problem."[6] As Creon says of Oedipus, the tragic heroes have "natures difficult for themselves to bear."

Despite this new inwardness, there is a sense in which the heroes are opaque to themselves, puzzled by who they really are. This is beautifully mirrored in the design of the Greek stage that suggests a tension between inside and outside, visible and hidden, public and private. All the visible action in Greek theater happens in front of a façade, most often the façade of a palace, but there is a door that leads to a hidden inside. Behind that door, completely hidden from view, many of the most important actions take place: recall, for example, Klytemnestra's murder of Agamemnon, Jocasta's suicide and Oedipus' self-blinding.[7]

The heroes of fifth-century tragedy are not just highly individualized characters, they are also paradigmatic figures, they are still *mythic.* This is yet another of the tensions so characteristic of this genre in its prime: Oedipus is not just a long-ago human individual but also a sacred king—and paradoxically, eventually, a sacred victim, a ritual scapegoat.

The dramatists seem to admire both *sophrosyne,* moderation, and the unbounded aspirations of so many of their protagonists—and expect us to wrestle with the same ambivalence. (I think of how as a young woman I was wholly in awe of Sophocles' Antigone and how now I have so many reservations about her and find myself more drawn to Ismene—and yet, and yet, the awe remains.)

Yet another example of the fundamentally paradoxical character of Greek tragedy is that despite its somewhat subversive questioning of conventional piety, most of the plays were performed as part of one of Athens most important annual religious festivals, the Dionysia, a six-day event celebrated in March or April at the theater of Dionysos with priests of Dionysos in attendance. (Some were performed instead at the Lenaia, a four-day festival in January or February also in honor of Dionysos.) Attendance at the *Dionysia* was a ritual, communal obligation. The law courts were closed; all public business was suspended. The audience at this largest annual gathering in Athens was immense, somewhere between 15,000 and 17,000. It included citizens, slaves, and foreigners, though there is no agreement among scholars as to whether or not it included women.

A festival celebrating the arrival of spring, the Dionysia opened with a re-enactment of the annual return of Dionysos; his statue was brought from a temple outside the city to the theater at its center. The festival opened with contests between chorus groups representing the city's ten tribes, followed by an honoring of persons who had significantly served the city during the preceding year, and a parading of the city's war orphans. All this civic self-congratulatory celebration was followed by the plays—which also said something about the city, albeit more transgressively. On three successive mornings one of the three poets who had been chosen in an earlier competition presented three tragedies plus a satyr play (a burlesque treatment of mythic themes which may have signified more explicitly than did the tragedies the relation of what was happening on the stage to Dionysos). The afternoons were devoted to the comedies—plays set in the present that often included harsh ridicule of living persons and trenchant political satire, along with lots of sexual and excremental humor (thus preserving an important aspect of Dionysian ritual absent from tragedy). Thus the comedies like the tragedies invited the polis to look at itself critically—though we know of no author who wrote both tragedy and comedy.

As part of a public religious festival tragedy validated the social order; at the same time its radical questioning of both divine and human justice challenged that order. This tension between context and content, this making of a ritual place for criticism, seems to be one of Greek tragedy's most important features.[8]

While set in the past, the tragedies were in significant ways about the present. Almost all were derived from the mythological tradition, except for Aeschylus' *Persians*, based on the Greek victory over the Persians at Salamis, a battle in which Aeschylus and many in his audience had fought. This victory was generally viewed in Athens as a triumph of the forces of liberty against despotism (much like the Allied victory in World War Two) yet Aeschylus dared to present the defeated enemy sympathetically, to show the fear and grief suffered by the Persian king's mother and the king's own lonely despair. But in the Peloponnesian War in which Greek was pitted against Greek (and which dragged on for most of the period during which the extant tragedies were first performed) it was less easy to see any clear moral distinction between the opponents—and perhaps just because of that these wars aroused a degree of passionate identification with the Athenian side that seems to have made it impossible to explicitly explore how Athens' own imperial ambitions had triggered and sustained the conflict. (Perhaps because historical writing did not evoke the immediate pull to emotional response of dramatic performance, the historian Thucydides could do what the tragedians couldn't, and so, toward the end of the war when it was already clear that Athens would in all likelihood lose, could Aristophanes in his *Lysistrata*.) In any case the tragedians found it was more effective (and perhaps safer) to use stories from the mythical past.

More recent historical events seemed too near and too familiar. To write of them would not allow for the aesthetic distancing so central to art's cathartic power, to the transposition of pity and terror onto a different plane. The tragedians needed the freedom to reimagine and reshape that a perhaps feared demand for historical accuracy would have inhibited. The turn to the legendary past made possible the recognition and exploration of the chaos underlying the present fragile social and religious order. So Euripides could present the suffering of the defeated Trojans, particularly the surviving Trojan wives and children, sympathetically, but not contemporary Spartans, could make visible the hubristic arrogance of the victorious Greeks of Homer's world but not that of his own fellow-citizens.

Indeed, the stories the tragedians told were set not only in a different time, but almost always in a different place as well, in a distant *elsewhere*—in Thebes, in Corinth, in Mycenae, not in Athens. Often Athens becomes the scene of whatever reconciliation or resolution the play might offer, as, for example, in the *Oresteia, Oedipus at Colonus,* and the *Medea.*

Thus the dramatists use the myths to call to a deeper, more resilient and more complex relation to the polis, and to the gods, to fate, suffering, and death. They use them to reflect on perennial but newly pressing issues. Tragedy stands at the intersection of two opposing relationships to myth; it neither accepts them uncritically nor dismisses them as false and harmful (as Plato for instance does in the next century). It uses and revisions them, often to question, even negate, the values the traditional versions upheld. The role of myth has changed: the meaningful no longer incontrovertible.

The tragedies are based on myths which the audience could be counted on to know well; the characters were figures from what they thought of as their own historical past *and* symbols of their own hopes and fears. The myths surround the plays, not only as the source of the plots, but as the before and after of the part of the story presented on stage, and as alternate versions of the same story which provide a kind of commentary on the new version. The dramatist could count on his audience catching his implicitly ironic view of his characters when he showed them knowing less of what was really going on around them than the spectators, familiar with the whole plot, did. Also, the many direct allusions within the plays to other myths add metaphorical depth to the particular story being retold. (And, of course, the plays shape how the myths will thenceforward be remembered.)

Just as tragedy represents a new kind of spectacle introduced into the polis's religious festivals, so, too, it represents a radically new literary genre, different from epic and lyric as well as from the rituals out of which it emerged. Drama reveals the ambiguities and anomalies present in the situations it represents. As it shows how each character has his or her own viewpoint, own hopes and fears, *we* keep being pulled back and forth between different perspectives, different identifications. For drama, as I've already noted, is *agon*, struggle, conflict. *Agon* is both the context and the subject of tragedy. The tragic performances (like the Olympian games) were competitive as well as religious events. A group of citizens chosen by lot voted to decide which dramatist, which actor, and which chorus deserved to win that year's first prize and which had come in second.

It is important to recognize how different drama is from epic's orderly eventoned narrative and from lyric's expression of personal feeling. Because the situations enacted on the stage are so much more pressing than those accessible to the lyric writer, there is an enormous increase in emotional intensity. In its power to evoke the presence of the transcendent tragedy is thus closer to ritual. Tragedy provides direct confrontation with individuals in crisis, in situations requiring action, even when all alternatives have their downside and it is clearly impossible to foresee all their consequences. The artificially dramatic situations in which the protagonists of tragedy find themselves characters are more than personal misfortunes; they raise big questions about the nature of justice, of the right order of things. These crises force self-reflection and thus a new sense of interiority and agency.

The enormous size of the audience and the consequent distance of most of the spectators from the stage (and the masks) meant that characterization was radically dependent on language, on speech. (Think of how different this is from the reliance in our theaters, and even more in our cinema, on facial expression and nuanced gestures.) In Greek tragedy the action is primarily mediated through dialogue, or perhaps it would be better to say through failed dialogue, through *mis*communication. The actors talk at one another and misunderstand each other. They use the same words but with different meanings in mind. (In the *Oresteia*, for example, just about everyone claims to have *dike*, justice, on their side.) Tragedy makes visible the ambiguity and opacity of language. (Think of the important roles played by the Sphinx's riddling language and the misleading oracles brought back from Delphi in *Oedipus the King.)*

In tragedy we also have a different relationship between writing and orality than in bardic or lyric performance. The texts of the plays were written (for the sake of the actors and chorus members who had to rehearse and learn their lines) and then spoken. It amazes me to realize that the original assumption was that these plays would only be performed *once,* at the festival for which they had been commissioned. It seems only to have been in the fourth century that they were replayed in Athens and elsewhere and that they were available to be *read* and not only seen and heard. Thus in the fourth century we could say they had become "plays," abstracted from their original ritual and social context, available to be understood in the way that my teachers fifty years ago understood them. That these plays are available to us at all is thus wholly due to those rehearsal texts!

But in the fifth century tragedy was an oral performance based on a written text. In drama there is no single voice of truth as there is in both epic and lyric, because the dramatist is not visibly present as the bard or lyrist is. (Although early on—before Sophocles—the dramatists did participate as actors. John Gould speculates that Aeschylus himself may have played Klytemnestra in the *Agamemnon*.[9]) What happens on stage does not issue from a single authoritative voice but from multiple voices. Tragic language creates ambiguity, dissolution not clarification.

Although there has been much speculation about the antecedents of the genre (going back to Aristotle's *Poetics*) there is almost no reliable information about what lies behind its emergence in fifth century Athens. We do know that the word *tragoidos* means "goat singer" and probably refers to goatskin-dressed performers of choral lyric (and that "comedy" derives from *komos*, a word describing a procession of revelers parading around with Dionysos' phallus). So it seems safe to assume that tragedy emerged from choral performances that were part of Dionysian ritual. And it's not difficult to discern the persistence of the ritual pattern of suffering-sacrifice-renewal in tragedy. Or to recognize remnants of ritual in the choral dances, the musical accompaniment, the masks, the stylized gestures, that were part of tragic performance. But tragedy is significantly different from ritual. The emphasis on innovation, on telling the familiar story in a new and unexpected way means that tragedy is by definition critical and transformative, whereas ritual is by definition conservative.

The time of transition to individual actors is unclear. The word for actor, *hypokrites*, means answerer or interpreter, which suggests that to begin with there was a responsive engagement between a single actor and the chorus. And even in Aeschylus we see much of the action still taking place in interchanges between a single actor and the chorus. But Aeschylus is credited with the introduction of the second actor, and Sophocles with the introduction of the third, and from then on it is the scenes involving interaction among the actors that move the action forward.

But: there's still a chorus, and it's not an anachronistic survival. The chorus is an essential and distinctive feature of Attic drama (even though Aristotle doesn't regard it as important enough to discuss). Indeed, the figures whom we speak of as the dramatists or the tragedians were in the fifth century called "chorus masters." The chorus, composed of ordinary citizens not professional actors, serves as representative of the citizen body, of the audience gathered in the theater. When the chorus becomes minimized (as it does in the fourth century) the change marks the end of one of the tensions particular to the genre in its prime, the tension between the individualized actors and the chorus. As Daniel Mendelsohn observes, what the presence of the chorus establishes is that "the ostensibly personal decisions made by the individual characters are always made in the setting of and always affect the larger society."[10] (Think of the plague in *Oedipus the King*.) The chorus is on stage throughout the play; the actors come and go. Everything happens in its presence, all experience has a public dimension; all action affects the community and not only the individual. The chorus carries memory—memory of the past that lies behind the present action, memory of other analogous stories. It carries the culture's collective memory, its mythic inheritance, and thus brings a wider perspective to bear.[11]

The form of tragedy involves a complex interplay between the choral and actor parts. Each is related both to the world of the past and to the present, but in opposite ways. The actors, though they represent characters from the long-ago heroic world, speak in Attic dialect and in a meter close to prose, close to the language of everyday discourse, thereby implying the relevance of what is happening on the stage to the contemporary world. The choral songs, which comment on the action and separate the scenes, are composed in lyric meters and in a Doric dialect, which evokes a more distant mythic world. And yet, because the chorus is composed of ordinary citizens, of one's neighbors, it, too, suggests the relevance of what is being performed to the contemporary world.

Yet it is important to understand (*contra* the established view a generation ago) that the chorus has no privileged perspective; it does not represent the poet's perspective or *the* meaning of the play—or even the presumed viewpoint of the assembled spectators. Usually the chorus within the play represents a marginalized not an authoritative social group—old men, women, slaves, foreigners. They speak as "I," not "we"—as having a collective identity that occasionally at moments of great tension becomes fractured. They are responding *within* the action and try moment by moment to make sense of it. Present throughout the play; they cannot escape from what is going on, but they are still there at the end—and in this and other ways represent the spectators who are also trying to make sense, moment by moment, of what is happening before them. Though it is important to realize that of course there was no univocal audience response. There was never—even at the first performance—a meaning attributable to the play being presented. (A relevant parallel would be how in the *Antigone* Antigone, Creon, and Haemon can each assume that the city agrees with them! Another would be how in the *Eumenides* the citizens of the jury divide equally between condemning and exonerating Orestes, so that Athene has to cast the deciding vote.)

This conviction that tragedy leaves things open, raises questions rather than resolving them, illuminates the complexities and contradictions rather than hiding them, is at the heart of how Greek tragedy is being viewed today in comparison with fifty years ago. This recognition of tragedy's focus on paradox, contradiction, and tension recovers its connection to the realm of Dionysos—the preeminently paradoxical god, masculine and feminine, Olympian and chthonic, creative and destructive. It seems stunningly fitting that Attic tragedy should essentially end with the *Bacchae*—with its explicit exploration of the destructive energies associated with this god and the greater destruction risked in denying him, and with its implicit celebration of art's sublimating power.

In tragedy myth became a mirror in which the classical polis could look at itself; its purpose was to develop a tragic consciousness in the spectators, an awareness of simultaneously valid contradictory perspectives. "The city turned itself into a theater—whose subject was itself."[12] Tragedy turns civic life into a problem, a riddle, a question; it reflects the anxieties and disagreements of its audience, and reveals the violence and irrationality that lay just below the surface of civic order and harmony. Its aim was to make the citizenry aware of the limitations and precariousness of the civic and religious order, not to criticize the polis order as such as the necessary basis for civilization but to criticize its dominant ideology, to express a hope—not an assurance—of the triumph of order and justice. Thus tragedy can suggest a more supple complex understanding of civic life and of the self.

There are ways, I believe, in which these tragedies might serve as a mirror in which we, too, might view ourselves. I don't mean that Greek tragedy offers us resolutions for our current dilemmas nor that there are neat parallels between its world and ours. We have no comparable public forum where criticism is part of our communal self-celebration. But I do believe that art, stories, myth, drama can open the imagination to see things more complexly—more from a soul than ego perspective—than other modes of expression. And perhaps—just as the abstraction from the present, the revisioning of their past, made it possible for the Greeks to look at their present more complexly—so our re-engagement with these tragedies, this literature from our past, might make it possible for us to look at our historical hour in a more multifaceted way. Sometimes the indirect speaks more directly to the soul.

Tragedy leaves things open; it helps us appreciate a multiplicity of perspectives, helps us acknowledge the intricacy of the historical situations we find ourselves in, the inadequacy of simplistic moral dualisms, the dangers of fundamentalisms and hubristic assertiveness. Goldhill, in what I find a wonderful analogy, suggests that the critic (or any of us) who tries to define tragedy is like Pentheus trying to bind Dionysos: It can't be done![13] We are given the possibility of opening ourselves to the continually unsettling and challenging questions set in motion by these plays—not only to reflect on what the plays mean but to reflect on how these questions are pertinent—and still troubling—in our own world. As Nicole Loraux once observed, "There is no statement about Athens…that does not nourish very contemporary passions."[14]

Notes

1. In Martin Buber, *Pointing the Way* (New York: Harper & Row, 1974).

2. Probably the most well known example of this approach is H. D. F. Kitto's *Greek Tragedy: A Literary Study,* originally published in 1939; Barnes & Noble published a revised edition in 1950.

3. Simon Goldhill, *Reading Greek Tragedy* (Cambridge: Cambridge University Press, 1999) 188.

4. Jean-Pierre Vernant and Pierre Vidal-Naquet, *Myth and Tragedy in Ancient Greece* (New York: Zone Books, 1988) 29.

5. See Goldhill, ch. 8.

6. Vernant, 25.

7. Froma Zeitlin, "Playing the Other," in John J, Winkler and Froma I. Zeitlin, *Nothing To Do With Dionysos? Athenian Drama in Its Social Context* (Princeton: Princeton University Press, 1990) 71, 75.

8. Charles Segal, *Interpreting Greek Tragedy: Myth, Poetry, Text* (Ithaca: Cornell University Press, 1986) 25.

9. John Gould, *Myth, Ritual, Memory, and Exchange: Essays in Greek Literature and Culture* (Oxford: Oxford University Press, 2001) 193.

10. Daniel Mendelsohn, "When Not in Greece," *New York Review of Books*, March 28, 2002, 35.

11. See the fine discussion in Gould, ch. 18.

12. Vernant, 33.

13. Goldhill, 285.

14. Nicole Loraux, *The Children of Athena* (Princeton: Princeton University Press, 1993) 250.

9

The Landscape of H.D.'s Mythic Imagination

As I began to think about what I might focus on in this year's lecture I realized that none thus far had related to one of my favorites among the courses I used to teach at SDSU: Religion and Literature. Once I saw that, I knew immediately that I'd like to find a way of sharing my love for the American Imagist poet, Hilda Doolittle, who wrote under the pen-name H.D.

I first discovered H.D. when I was a freshman in college in the anthology of twentieth century American poets used in our introductory English course. The assignments directed us to Robert Frost, T. S. Eliot, Ezra Pound, William Carlos Williams, Wallace Stevens—but tucked away among these "important men" were Marianne Moore, Amy Lowell, and H.D.—and it was H.D. who won my heart.

It soon became evident to me that to talk about H.D. was to return to many of the themes I've touched upon in earlier lectures: my love of Greece and especially my fascination with Greek tragedy, the Holocaust, the Torah, Freud, feminism, bisexuality, goddesses. Not that I could hope really to explore all these connections in one brief hour!

Yet I do believe that by structuring my presentation around the ways in which the landscape of ancient Greece—imagined, visited, remembered—nurtured her poetry and her soul I can at least approach many of them. "What are the islands to me, What is Greece?"[1] She asks and I find myself wanting to trace the history of her changing response to that question.

Initially H.D. turns to Greece—its landscape, its myths, its poetry—in order to illuminate personal feeling; later it helps her express the painful complexities of interpersonal relationships, especially the relationships between women and men; finally she finds in it resources for a vision of a collective healing. In the poems she writes in the period just before the First World War, H.D. uses images drawn from the Greek landscape to communicate the eternal presentness of seemingly momentary experience. Later, during the 1920s, she uses the stories and figures of Greek myth to explore some of the most painful conflicts and disappointments of her personal life. Retelling the myths from a woman's perspective, she reveals their often-ignored misogyny and suggests how omnipresent and crippling that misogyny still is. Then her analysis with Freud in 1933 and 1934 introduces her to the world of the more ancient mother goddesses and she learns that "under every altar to Zeus…there is an earlier altar." This leads her to a new belief in the possibility of gathering up long-scattered mythic shards to create a new vision and to a new confidence in the power of poetry to bring healing both to shattered selves and to a shattered world.

Let me begin with "H.D., Imagist" and her relation to an *imagined* Greece. This means beginning with a story. The story is set in the British Museum in London. It is August 1912. Ezra Pound and Hilda Doolittle are both in their twenties, two young Americans living in England. They are engaged. She shows him a poem she has just written, called "Hermes of the Ways." "But, dryad, this is poetry!" he exclaims. He slashes out some lines, indicates cuts with his pencil, then scrawls "H.D., Imagiste" at the bottom of the page.

Shortly after this encounter H.D. learns of Pound's involvement with another woman, Dorothy Shakespear, and breaks off their engagement. In her 1921 novel *Paint it Today* (which remains unpublished) H.D. describes her relation to Pound in these words:

> She had parted with the youth, having gained nothing from him but a feeling that someone had tampered with an oracle, had banged on a temple door, had dragged out small, curious, sacred ornaments, had not understood their inner meaning, yet with a slight sense of their inner value, their perfect tint and carving, had not stolen them, but left them, perhaps worse, exposed by the roadside, reft from their shelter, and their holy setting.[2]

We might say that, like Hermes the thief, Pound had stolen her poetry, although the poetic voice in her 1916 collection *Sea Garden* seems clearly to be a woman's voice, the voice of a woman who wants to be both woman and poet, not Pound's muse or his creation. The poetry she writes during this period is in part a sublimation of her love for him and expressive of her desolation at being rejected, but it also represents a kind of subjugation to him. It was Pound who *defined* "Imagism," her way of writing poetry. Imagism, he said, meant a harder, nearer to the bone "crystallized" lyric poetry, which focuses on instantaneousness, on images which present an intellectual and emotional complex in an instant of time and thus express a sense of sudden liberation from the constrictions of time and space.

H.D.'s Imagist poems, the poems in *Sea Garden*, though pastoral, are set in an unusually wild and harsh landscape. They are often set in Greece—but Greece here means a landscape of the imagination. H.D. had never yet been to Greece; the landscape of these poems is actually modeled on childhood memories of the New England coast, but imaginally the landscape is Greek because already for her Greece is the soul's homeland.

The rugged natural landscape serves as a correlate for the landscape of H.D.'s soul and body, provides her with a way of locating her own individual experience, of finding herself, not of accessing the archetypal universal aspects of that experience but of entering into its particularity. The natural world provides her with a way of both entering into her own turmoil and distancing herself from it by seemingly speaking only of broken flowers and trampled reeds. As a contemporary reviewer wrote: "The unpracticed reader, picking up H.D.'s *Sea Garden* and reading it casually, might suppose it was all about flowers and rocks and waves and Greek myths, when it is really about the soul."[3]

This is evident in almost every poem, as in these lines from "Sea Iris":

> Weed, moss-weed,
> root tangled in sand,
> sea-iris, brittle flower,
> one petal like a shell
> is broken,
> and you print a shadow
> like a thin twig.[4]

or these from "Sea Lily":

> Reed,
> slashed and torn
> but doubly rich—
> such great heads as yours
> drift upon temple-steps,

> but you are shattered
> in the wind.[5]

or these from "Oread":

> Whirl up, sea—
> Whirl your pointed pines,
> Splash your great pines
> On our rocks,
> Hurl your green over us,
> Cover us with pools of fir.[6]

Note the verbs: tangled, broken, slashed, torn, shattered, whirl, splash, hurl. Note the emphasis on the excitement of places where opposed elements meet: reed and wind, pine and sea, wave and anemone. This is not Symbolism. These poems present a situation. They do not represent it. We might say that they dissolve the subject-object distinction, suggest that emotions are not only subjective but also objective, occur not only in the soul but also in the natural world. Nor are they poems of desire; they don't lead outside themselves, don't express a longing that the tensions be resolved. Rather, they hold the tension, present it as occurring for all eternity, as what *is*.

A poem like "Hermonax" reveals H.D.'s close, attentive observation of a rock-strewn beach *and* conveys her defensiveness, her sadness, loneliness, vulnerability, and estrangement, her uprootedness—perhaps more than she herself consciously realizes:

> Broken by great waves
> The wavelets flung it here,
> This sea-gliding creature like a weed
> Covered with salt foam,
> Torn from the hillocks of rock.[7]

It is not difficult to recognize the connections between these poems and events in H.D.'s life at the time of their composition. Shortly after her break with Pound she marries the English poet Richard Aldington and then after the war erupts enters into an impassioned, intimate (though probably not sexually consummated) relationship with D.H. Lawrence. Time and again she finds herself dependent on male mentors—Pound, Aldington, Lawrence—men who tended to see her as their disciple, their creation.

In these early years H.D. seems to want both to be "one of the boys" (recognized as a poet in her own right) and loved as a desirable/desiring woman. She sees the world of the poetic tradition as the world of the fathers, herself as poet as in touch with a masculine side of herself. She is deeply disappointed when she discovers how for Pound and Lawrence the relationship falls into the typical dominating man-objectified woman pattern—how for them she is "painted like a fresh prow."[8]

The marriage with Aldington seems initially to have been a joy-filled one. But then the war breaks out; H.D. gives birth to a stillborn child and her marriage falls apart. Aldington has an affair. She is deeply disappointed by his infidelity, by his enthusiasm for war, his neglect of his art. Again she feels herself caught in a male-defined world, as her poem "Sheltered Garden" clearly expresses:

> I have had enough.
> I gasp for breath.
>
> . . . . . .
>
> I have had enough—
>
> . . . .
>
> O to blot out this garden
> to forget, to find a new beauty
> in some terrible
> wind-tortured place.[9]

So then she turns to Lawrence—and suffers the same disappointment, a disappointment powerfully communicated in her poem "Eurydice":

> So you have swept me back,
> I who could have walked with the live souls
> above the earth.
> I who could have slept among the live flowers
> at last.
>
> so for your arrogance
> and your ruthlessness
> I am swept back

> where dead lichens drip
> dead cinders upon moss of ash.[10]

A disappointment, a deep-seated grief and a sense of having lost herself with her loss of his love, is also communicated in lines from the poem with which I began this exploration but didn't quote then: "What are the islands to me? What is Greece?" she begins, and then goes on, "What are the islands to me if you are lost?"[11]

This sense of loss is further aggravated by her feeling that the war had shattered the world, her world. "The war will never be over," she writes. She means the literal war but also perhaps the war between men and women, and the inner war between herself as dependent/vulnerable woman and as creative poet.

Her brother was killed in the war and her father dies in grief over his death. Her relationship with Lawrence ends and so, to all effect, does her marriage with Aldington. She has a brief affair. It ends. She finds herself pregnant, alone, and deathly ill with the influenza that killed so many in 1919. She is near breakdown; and then Bryher appears.

Bryher is the pen-name of Winifred Ellerman, the slightly younger, immensely rich woman with whom H.D. lived for most of the rest of her life. Before Bryher ever met H.D., she was already in love with her poems. Indeed, she had memorized *Sea Garden*. Bryher finds H.D. in Cornwall when the life of both mother and unborn child were in serious danger; she sees her safely through Perdita's birth and then takes her to Greece.

When H.D. begins to write poetry again Greece is still central, but it is a different Greece, not so much the landscape as the stories, the figures, the Greece of the ancient poets. Because she saw the war as having shattered the intensely esthetic world of Imagism and its implicitly narcissistic emphasis on individual feeling, in the poetry that she writes during the 1920s, it becomes more important to speak directly about the conflicts that occur between persons and not only to allude to those that take place within the soul, and to speak more directly as well about the wish that these conflicts, especially those between women and men, might be resolved—and about her despair of this happening.

But it is still Greece that provides her with the images and words to say what she needs to say. As she had written in 1918:

> Greece is indeed the tree-of-life, the ever-present stream, the spring of living
> water.... I know that we need scholars to decipher and interpret the Greek,

but we also need poets and mystics and children to rediscover the Hellenic world, to see *through* the words the words being the outline, the architectural structure of that door or window, through which we are all free, scholar and unlettered alike, to pass.[12]

The poems of this period communicate H.D.'s discovery of a coalescence between the ancient stories and her own most intensely painful conflicts. James Hillman has said, "Myths do not tell us how, they simply give us the invisible background which starts us imagining, questioning, going deeper."[13] To which I would add, myths do not necessarily heal or bring comfort either. Certainly for H.D. the myths she retold weren't comforting or healing; rather they confirmed her own experiences of grief and rage.

During this period she devotes much energy to translations, re-vision-ed versions, interpretations, amplifications of classical Greek poetry. She retells the ancient myths differently, from a woman's perspective. Her poems give voice to the women objectified in the inherited male-centered versions. She finds Greece can serve a radical decentering of patriarchal heterosexism. She sets Greek against Greek; the male poetic tradition against her version (and that of Sappho and Euripides).

Not too surprisingly, she's especially drawn to Sappho, and writes several poems based on Sappho fragments. For instance her version of Sappho's Fragment Thirty Six (*I know not what to do/my mind is divided*) begins

> I know not what to do,
> my mind is reft:
> is song's gift best?
> is love's gift loveliest?

Thus for H.D. this becomes yet another poem about the conflict she experiences between her desire to be a poet and her longing to love and be loved.

But H.D. was also drawn to Euripides whom she describes as "a white rose, lyric, feminine, a spirit."[14] She translates parts of his *Iphigenia in Aulis, Ion, Hecuba, Hippolytus,* and the *Bacchae,* and writes poems deeply indebted to his *Hippolytus,* and his *Helen.* In these adaptations H.D. speaks the language of Greek myth to explore her own story, her sense of betrayal by the male poets she had loved and the conflict she experiences between her own passion and need and her desire for autonomy and creativity.

Among my favorites of these revisionings is her *Hippolytus Temporizes.* Although H.D. begins by claiming this is the familiar story of Theseus, Hippolyta, and Phaedra, we soon discover it doesn't seem familiar at all. The verse is not surprisingly very much H.D.'s own: not Euripides' measured Greek hexameter but the jagged irregular lines H.D. uses to express the effect of overpowering emotion. Often each line contains but a single word, repeated over and over.

But the story, too, is changed. Theseus, hated here by both Hippolyta and Phaedra, never appears. Nor does Aphrodite. H.D. gives us an Artemis who wants nothing to do with human worshippers:

> I heard the intolerable rhythm
> And sound of prayer,
> So I have hidden
> Where no mortals are.

And a Hippolytus who pursues Artemis as a substitute for the Amazon mother who died in giving birth to him. This Hippolytus loves Artemis's wild and fierce natural world *and her,* wants a contact she refuses:

> Artemis
> Artemis
> . . . .
>
> I have implored the adder
> and the bear,
> the lynx,
> the pard,
> the panther
> for some prayer,
> some charm,
> some peril to entrap your feet
> . . . .
>
> hot, hot in my desire
> to trace you in the forest,
> in the brake,
> in the tangle of wild larch.[15]

H.D.'s Phaedra hates the coldness of Greece and her old, old husband; she longs for the sensuousness and warmth of her Cretan homeland. So we understand how easily Aphrodite fills her with longing for her beautiful young stepson. We have already sensed that Hippolytus's devotion to Artemis has a strongly aphroditic flavor which might make him more open to Phaedra than he could ever consciously acknowledge. So we are almost ready for H.D.'s marvelous twist: Phaedra comes to him disguised as Artemis and he is completely taken in, delirious with joy at having his goddess finally yield to him. Unwilling to accept that he has been deceived, and when finally forced to, completely undone.

As we read the play we see how H.D. has herself entered into each of these figures: into Hippolytus with his love of nature at its most fierce, into Artemis and her wish to be recognized as who she *is* rather than to be desired or possessed, and into Phaedra and her profound unhappiness, her deep-seated homesickness and sense of being cut-off from all that is life-giving. And we see that for H.D. tragedy seems the inevitable outcome of these conflicts.

Among her many other poems on Greek themes that H.D. writes during this period are powerful ones about Calypso, Circe, Helen, about how these women were used and abused by men. Yet for H.D. these poems were in some way a dead-end; they didn't help move her forward, beyond her despair, her confusion, her rage. With the exception of the "Demeter" poem which ends:

> *What of her—*
> *mistress of Death—*
> *what of his kiss?*
> Ah, strong were his arms to wrest
> slight limbs from the beautiful earth,
> young hands that plucked the first
> buds of the chill narcissus
> and fingers that broke
> and fastened the thorny stalk
> with the flower of wild acanthus.
>
> Ah, strong were the arms that took
> (ah, evil the heart and graceless),
> but the kiss was less passionate![16]

I find in these lines a conviction that mother-daughter love is more fundamental than sexual love, than man-woman love, and an intimation of a figure who will become more and more important to H.D. (especially after her analysis with Freud) of a divine mother who contains Artemis's inviolability and Aphrodite's sensuousness.

During this period H.D. also writes many novels, most of which remained unpublished during her lifetime, probably because of the lesbian ambiance of much of this prose. The turn to fiction may have been motivated by her wish to get over being "their" H.D., the Imagist poet, but the prose, like the poetry, focuses on tangled unsatisfying relationships, on resolved tensions, on pain. And, as she later realizes, there was evasion in her focus on love (the accepted female theme) and avoidance of war (the male topic) and so a failure to address much of what had led to her World War I breakdown.

And so she makes her way to Freud. Her discontent with the writing of this period is not exactly writer's block since she keeps writing—but she experiences this writing as sterile, repetitive, compliant. H.D.'s overt reason for coming to Freud in 1933 is fear sparked by the rise of Nazism and the threat it represented of a new war. She recognizes the need to confront how those fears arose from her unworked-through experience of the 1914–18 war.

H.D.'s experience of her work with Freud is beautifully communicated in her retrospective memoir, *Tribute to Freud,* written well after Freud's death, partly in London during the war and partly in Kusnacht a decade later, and in her poem "The Master" written while she was still in Vienna but not published until years after her death. Only a few months ago Susan Stanford Friedman published a more private and more informal account of this period in H.D.'s life, *Analyzing Freud: Letters of H.D., Bryher, and Their Circle*[17]—invaluable not only for the additional light it sheds on the "collaboration" between H.D. and Freud but also for the access it gives us to a deeper understanding of the relationship between H.D. and Bryher, which is often obscured in biographies which focus on H.D.'s relationship to one of the men in her life, Pound or Lawrence or Freud.

It is important that she comes to Freud when she does, after he had discovered what he called the Minoan-Mycenaean layer of the unconscious, after he had come to recognize the power of the pre-Olympian, pre-Oedipal mother, after he had acknowledged the enduring importance for women of their primal bond with their mothers. "He said at the very beginning I had come to find my mother."[18]

In the transference, H.D. finds Freud is both mother and father. He keeps making her return to *that* relationship, kept trying to help her recover the original strong emotional connection that had bound her to her mother. She finds that this rediscovery of her mother frees her to relate to her own woman self, to accept being a woman as she never fully had before, and helps her accept a bisexuality about which she has always been ambivalent and confused.

Freud also brings her to the Mother Goddess and helps her discover how we often have to go back behind father symbols to recover the primal mother, source of birth:

> Mary, Mara, Miriam, Mut,
>
> Madre, Mere, Mother, pray for us...
>
> This is Gaia, this is the beginning.
>
> This is the end,
>
> Under every shrine to Zeus, to Jupiter,
>
> to Theus-pater, or God-the-father...
>
> there is an earlier altar.[19]

Thus Freud introduces H.D to yet a different Greece, a more ancient Greece, the Greece of the mother goddesses, a Greece intimately connected to the yet more ancient world of Egypt. The analysis itself took place in the world of myth. H.D. experiences Freud as midwife to the soul, as Asclepius the blameless physician, as an Orpheus who charms the very beasts of the unconscious and enlivens the dead sticks and stones of buried thoughts and memories, as an old Hermit who lives on the edge of the great forest of the unknown, as a trickster-thief nonchalantly unlocking vaults and caves, taking down the barriers that generations had carefully set up, as Faust, as a Prometheus stealing fire from heaven, as the curator in a museum of priceless antiquities.

"The Professor said we two met in our love of antiquity."[20] So where was it that they met? In Vienna? In Greece? In Egypt? In *Tribute to Freud* H.D. describes her first visit to Freud's consulting room:

> No one had told me that this room was lined with treasures. I was to greet the Old Man of the Sea, but no one had told me of the treasures he had salvaged from the sea-depth...He is at home here. He is part and parcel of these treasures. I have come a long way. I have brought nothing with me.... He is the infinitely old symbol, weighing the soul, Psyche, in balance. Does the Soul, passing the portals of life, entering the House of Eternity, greet the Keeper of

the Door? It seems so. I should have thought the Door-Keeper, at home beyond the threshold, might have greeted the shivering soul. Not so, the Professor. But waiting & finding that I would not or could not speak, he uttered. What he said—and I thought a little sadly—was, "You are the only person who has ever come into this room and looked at the things in the room before looking at me."

But worse was to come. A little lion-like creature came padding toward me—a lioness, as it happened...I bend down to greet the creature. But the Professor says, "Do not touch her—she snaps—she is difficult with strangers." *Strangers?* Is the Soul crossing the threshold a stranger to the Door-Keeper?[21]

H.D. crouches on the floor and the chow nuzzles against her shoulder. "He is at home here," Freud remarks, and soon he lets her know he wants her to feel at home there, too. She comes to know the house as home and as the Cathedral. The "treasures," Freud's antiquities, become an important part of their work together. Decades earlier in a letter to Wilhelm Fliess Freud had called them his "gods." Years later Marie Bonaparte persuades the Nazis to allow Freud's collection to follow him to London. Shortly after their safe arrival, H.D. sends Freud magnolias and a card inscribed, "To greet the return of the gods."

H.D. speaks of one of their sessions as going "off on one of our journeys...this time it was Italy; we were together in Rome. The years went forward, then backward."[22] But more often they are in Greece. In Freud's Viennese consulting room in 1933 *and* in Greece in 1920. H.D. and Bryher are in a Corfu hotel bedroom. Projected on the wall, H.D. watches dim shapes forming, a series of hieroglyphs. A male silhouette, a goblet, a tripod. She is not sure whether it is her own hand or another's that is shaping these images. Watching them appear, encouraging their emergence, requires intense concentration and courage. She is not sure she can continue but Bryher encourages her, "Go on." A ladder appears and then a winged Nike figure. H.D. falls back, exhausted, but Bryher carries on and sees the Nike embraced by Helios, the sun god.

Time and time again in their sessions H.D. and Freud return to this scene which H.D. refers to as the "Writing on the Wall." She tells him how she had felt "that my whole life, my whole being, will be blighted forever if I miss this chance," and yet how thirteen years later she still doesn't understand this vision's meaning. She speaks of the years between as a seemingly endless period of waiting. At one point Freud gets up to bring her the little Athene figurine from his desk. "This is my favorite," he tells her, and she recognizes her winged Nike in his wingless Athene. Her Nike is *hers*, now—a victorious goddess, breaking free.

Almost as often as they journey to Greece, they go together to Egypt. On Freud's wall is an engraving of the temple at Karnak where she had been but Freud had not. On his desk next to the Athene are Egyptian figures, a Ra or Nut or Ka, a beautiful Osiris. During the time she is seeing him Freud is working on his Moses book and she learns from a mutual friend that Lawrence (whom she had not seen again in all those many years) had used her as the model for the priestess of Isis figure in his last book, *The Man Who Died*. One day Freud takes her to the other room, unlocks the glass-fronted cabinet and shows her his Sekmet, the fierce lion-headed daughter of Ra. And she tells him of her visit to the dark little temple off the great temple of Karnak and of seeing the great Sekmet hidden behind its locked doors. (As I first read this I couldn't help but remember my own visit to that same awesome Sekmet and also my visit to the Freud Museum in London and being taken by the curator to that same locked cabinet and being allowed to finger its as yet uncatalogued contents, holding in my hands that same tiny Sekmet figurine.)

In the most important dream she has during her analysis a princess, the Pharoah's daughter, is coming down steps leading to the river where she, the dreamer, stands guard over a child lying in a basket hidden among the bulrushes. Freud asks her whether she is Miriam or Moses. She comes to understand she is both, both woman and poet-prophet.

During their last sessions they return to Greece and to Egypt. The Professor tells her that Athene is the veiled Isis or Neith the warrior-goddess. He places the little statue of Athene in her hands. Together they remember the writing on the wall, the winged Victory, the Sekmet, Miriam and Moses.

Her poem "The Master" beautifully communicates what these journeys backward and forward meant to her:

> He was very beautiful,
> the old man,
> and I knew wisdom,
> I found measureless truth
> in his words.
>
> . . . . .
>
> (how did he understand?)
>
> . . . .
>
> I had two loves separate;
> God who loves all mountains

alone knew why
and understood
and told the old man
to explain
the impossible
which he did.

. . . . .

he will trouble the thoughts of men
yet for many an aeon—

. . . . . .

they will discuss all his written words...
and keep all his sacred writings safe

. . . . . .

they will found temples in his name

. . . .

only I,
I will escape

And it was he himself, he who set me free
to prophesy

he did not say
"stay,
be my disciple"—

. . . .

no,
he was rather casual,
"we won't argue about that"
(he said)
"you are a poet"

I said good-bye
and saw his old head
as he turned,
as he left the room

leaving me alone
with all his old trophies,
the marbles, the vases, the stone Sphinx,
the old, old jars from Egypt;
he left me alone with these things
and his old back was bowed.

The poem concludes with a paean of praise to the mother goddess to whom Freud had introduced her: "She is a woman, yet beyond woman, yet in woman." "No man will be present in those mysteries," she writes, "yet all men will kneel."[23]

After the analysis for most of H.D.'s life writing came freely, easily, despite the outbreak of that war she had so feared. He restored the lava flow. Her poetry is now a very different poetry, a poetry "growing within the grave," a poetry which seeks to bring healing to both a shattered self and the shattered world, a poetry which expresses hope not despair.

Snow falls on the desert;

it had happened before,
it would happen again.'[24]

The war *will* end.

As the bombs were falling on London, she writes a poem in praise of the God-dess as women know her, not the goddess of patriarchy, a poem in praise of a goddess "without any of the usual attributes," a goddess who

carries a book that is not
the tome of ancient wisdom.

the pages, I imagine, are the blank pages
of the unwritten volume of the new

a goddess who makes possible the emergence of "Psyche, the
butterfly, out of the cocoon."[25]

H.D. writes what many consider her most significant work, *Helen in Egypt,* in her sixties. What she now wants to say requires a different language from the compressed brevity of Imagism, requires an epic rather than a lyric form. But epic as H.D. writes it focuses not on heroic action but on introspection and reflection.

Helen in Egypt offers us a quest modeled on psychoanalysis, a woman's search for self through memory, interpretation, reflection and free association. The poetry of H.D.'s later years relies on dream:

> Now it appears very clear
> that the Holy Ghost,
>
> childhood's mysterious enigma
> is the Dream;
>
> that way of inspiration
> is always open,
> . . . .
> it explains symbols of the past
> in today's imagery,
>
> it merges the distant future
> with most distant antiquity.[26]

and on using mythic shards to make new poetry :

> steal then, O orator,
> plunder, O poet
> . . . .
> collect the fragments of splintered glass
> and of your fire and breath
> melt down and integrate,
> re-invoke, re-create
> opal, onyx, obsidian
> now scattered in the shards
> men tread upon.[27]

Myth no longer provides H.D. only with personae for her own contemporary experience but with connections to a collective unconscious. She now recognizes in myth the source of a potential collective healing.

Her Helen is not a passive victim of men's idealization or castigation. She is actively, creatively making a whole of the fragments of her life. She is healing herself and in so doing modeling healing of the war between women and men, a healing of a world torn asunder by our turning again and again to war as a way of dealing with conflict.

Like Euripides' *Helen*, H.D.'s *Helen in Egypt* is based on the tradition that the real Helen never went to Troy. While a phantom Helen was in Troy, the real Helen was in Egypt, waiting for Menelaus. But H.D.'s Helen, unlike Euripides's, can be in Troy and Egypt simultaneously. Her Helen is insistent on exploring her relation to the hated Helen, not just praying for Menelaus's return.

In trying to recover her buried self, she first calls upon the ghost of dead Achilles for his answers about the forgotten/repressed past, and then turns to her first lover, old Theseus (a figure clearly modeled on Freud) who helps her sort through her past to reconcile her various fragmented selves. So this Helen comes to remember her earlier selves without shame and can even confront the most deeply repressed memory of all, her most grievous violation of taboo, her abandonment of her daughter. She also begins to realize how the negative judgments have made her forget the joyous springtime love of early time with Paris.

The poem includes a lovely picture of old Theseus/Freud comforting Helen/H.D.:

> why do you weep, Helen?
> what cruel path have you trod?
> these heavy thongs
> let me unclasp them
>
> . . . .
> your feet are wounded
>
> . . . .
> will you choose from the cedar-chest there
> your own fleece-lined shoes?
> or shall I choose for you?[28]

H.D. died in 1961. On her gravestone are written the simple words: "Greek flower, Greek ecstasy."

Notes

Permission to quote H.D.'s poetry was given me by her daughter, Perdita Schaffner.

1. H.D., "The Islands," *Collected Poems 1912–1944* (New York: New Directions, 1983) 124.

2. Quoted in Janice S. Robinson, *H.D.: The Life and Work of an American Poet* (Boston: Houghton Mifflin, 1982) 40.

3. Quoted in Robinson, 70.

4. "Sea Iris," *Collected Poems*, 36.

5. "Sea Lily," *Collected Poems*, 14.

6. "Oread," *Collected Poems*, 55.

7. "Hermonax," *Collected Poems*, 58.

8. "Sea Iris," *Collected Poems*, 37.

9. "Sheltered Garden," *Collected Poems,* 19–21.

10. "Eurydice," *Collected Poems*, 51.

11. "The Islands," *Collected Poems*, 127.

12. From unpublished "Notes on Euripides," 1918, quoted in Robinson, 363, 365.

13. James Hillman, *ReVisioning Psychology* (New York: Harper & Row, 1975) 158.

14. H.D., *Notes on Thought and Vision* (San Francisco: City Lights, 1982) 32.

15. H.D., *Hippolytus Temporizes* (Boston: Houghtom Mifflin, 1927) 1, 4.15.

16. "Demeter," *Collected Poems*, 114f.

17. Susan Stanford Friedman, ed., *Analyzing Freud: Letters of H.D., Bryher, and Their Circle* (New York: New Directions, 2002).

18. H.D., *Tribute to Freud* (New York: McGraw-Hill, 1974) 17.

19. Quoted in Susan Stanford Friedman, *Psyche Reborn: The Emergence of H.D.* (Bloomington: Indiana University Press, 1981) 145, from the unpublished manuscript version of H.D.'s *The Gift*. Not included in the shortened version published in 1982 by New Directions.

20. *Tribute*, 175.

21. *Tribute*, 97, 98.

22. *Tribute*, 9.

23. "The Master," *Collected Poems*, 451–461.

24. "The Flowering Rod," *Collected Poems*, 605f.

25. "Tribute to the Angels," *Collected Poems*, 570.

26. "The Walls Do Not Fall," *Collected Poems*, 526.

27. "Tribute to the Angels," *Collected Poems*, 547f.

28. H.D. *Helen in Egypt* (New York: New Directions, 1961) 151f.

10

Looking Back at Orpheus

> And there they walk
> Together now; at times they are side by side;
> At times she walks ahead with him behind;
> At other times it's Orpheus who leads—
> But without any need to fear should he
> Turn round to see his own Eurydice.[1]

These lines from Ovid's account of Orpheus' reunion with Eurydice in Hades after his own death suggest that there is a kind of looking back that is creative, that comes from a suffering truly endured, and wholly different from the looking back shaped by an unwillingness to admit to the reality of loss and death. The body of Orpheus has just been dismembered, but the shade, the soul, of Orpheus, descending to the underworld, remembers all the places he had visited before. And we remember that Orpheus is a grandson of Mnemosyne, the Titan goddess of Memory and that, as is the case with all deities, her gifts can bring disaster or healing.

I have long been fascinated by Orpheus and by how the poets of ancient Greece and of our own world have kept remembering, reimagining, and recreating him—and now see how the myths about this gifted poet could help me make the last of these lectures a meditation in part on remembering, on the difference that Freud made so much of between repetition and remembrance. I have so valued these annual returns to SDSU and to the community I had to leave before I was really ready to—but ten years is enough, it's time now to remember, not keep repeating.

Some fifteen years ago I was invited to be the main speaker at a weekend conference at Pacifica Graduate Institute in Santa Barbara centered on the theme "Descending with Orpheus." Honoring my acceptance of that invitation meant missing the SDSU Commencement in which I was to be honored as the out-

126

standing faculty member. I had no idea then, of course, that in a sense this presaged my move from SDSU to Pacifica where I've been teaching these last ten years.

As I now turn back to returning to Orpheus for the first time since then I find myself amazed, as I always am when I return to a myth I think I already know, by how much more there is to this story than I had earlier recognized. Fifteen years ago it was Ovid's telling of the myth (and Rilke's amplification of that telling) which moved me most. Looking at the story from a woman's perspective, I saw an Orpheus who just didn't seem able to recognize that "his" Eurydice was precisely that, *his* Eurydice—and that Eurydice herself now really belonged in the underworld. Now I find myself wanting to give equal credit to Virgil's Orpheus, an Orpheus deeply in love with *her* and really not knowing how to live without her. I want to honor that *both* are true—and also want to move beyond an identification with Eurydice so unequivocal that it blinds me to my own relation to Orpheus.

Part of what delights me about myth is precisely this: that the same myth can be understood in so many different ways, depending on to what aspect, what episode, which figure, which version we choose to direct our focus. The more attentively we look the more we come to appreciate how each detail, each variant account, belongs, deepens, complicates.

I am also intrigued by how myths get reimagined over the centuries—how it was such reimagining that kept them alive in the ancient world—and that keeps them alive in ours. One of the distinctive features of the history of Greek mythology is that in Greece, as contrasted for instance with Egypt or Israel, the stories belonged to the poets not the priests. The dominance of Zeus, the articulation of the Olympian pantheon, the clear differentiation between the various gods and goddesses, was really more the work of Homer and the bards who preceded him than of cult.

Given that the myths belong to the poets, it is not at all surprising that there will be a myth about a poet: the myth of Orpheus. There is, of course, more to Orpheus than his being a poet but that is where this myth begins. That is the kernel out of which everything grows and around which everything else accretes. To understand the history of Orpheus thus requires dis-membering, and then re-membering, the myth.

In early Greece poets were regarded as having shamanic powers, as inspired by the gods, as magicians. Their chants, songs accompanied by the lyre, were incantation, enchantment. In this still predominantly oral culture the primary way to transmit traditional knowledge was through poetic speech. The poet's voice was honored as divinely inspired, as absolutely reliable and authoritative.

Orpheus seems to have been an especially intriguing figure to the poets since through their revisioning of him they could clarify their own experience of being poets. Almost inevitably Orpheus becomes associated with the primary themes to which they as poets are perennially drawn, love and death.

We don't really know how old the Orpheus myth is, though the Orphics of the fifth century BCE claimed it went far back—but Orpheus is absent from the epic literature, perhaps because the epic poets viewed themselves as muse-inspired bards. What we might ascribe to the imagination, Homer traces to an actual experience shared with him by the Muses who are everywhere and so know every-thing. Hesiod speaks of the muses teaching him beautiful singing, breathing their divine voice into him and warning him, "We know how to tell many falsehoods that seem real, but we also know how to speak truth when we wish to."[2] Even the sixth century archaic lyric poets make no mention of Orpheus, though for Sap-pho it is Aphrodite not the Muses who inspire her song.

Perhaps it is only in a slightly later period when, with the spread of literacy, the poets' claim of a supernatural origin for their words is liable to be viewed with suspicion that an Orpheus becomes necessary. The earliest references (which appear toward the end of the sixth century BCE) present Orpheus as coming from Thrace, where Greeks probably first came into contact with shamanic beliefs about birds and beasts summoned by a magician's song and about jour-neys to the underworld to recover stolen souls.[3] Thrace was also the traditional locus of the beginnings of Dionysian worship.

Thus from the outset there is an at least implicit connection between Orpheus and Dionysos. But Orpheus is also said to be a son of Apollo.[4] Indeed, it seems impossible to know whether Orpheus was initially an underworld daimon, a chthonic deity like Dionysos, or a follower of Apollo.[5] Thus taking the connec-tion to both deities seriously is somehow central. The myth about Orpheus is at least in part about the tension between the form-giving power of art associated with Apollo and the disruptive death-dealing power of passion associated with Dionysos. We will see that the myth can be—indeed, has been, read—in both ways: with art as triumphant or with death.

A close reading of the myth may also help us move beyond the too simple antithetical understanding of the relationship between Apollo and Dionysos fos-tered by a misreading of Nietzsche. The Delphic Apollo is quite Dionysian; the Orphic Dionysos quite Apollonian! Both Apollo and Dionysos are associated with music: Apollo with the lyre, whose sweet melody is ideally suited to accompany song; Dionysos with the aulos, the double pipes whose emotionally stirring sounds tend to drown out the human voice.

Apollo, it is said, gave Orpheus the lyre that Hermes had long ago given him. According to the "Homeric Hymn to Hermes," the infant god, born in the morning, played the lyre by afternoon. Sneaking out of his cradle, he spied a turtle and immediately had the idea of using its shell to make himself a musical instrument. A few minutes later he cleverly arranges to steal Apollo's cattle and then manages to soothe his older brother's justified anger over the theft by playing the lyre. "Cow-killer," Apollo says to him, "I think our differences can be settled peaceably. My heart has never been so struck by anything as it has by this," "So I'll give it you," Hermes responds, "but remember: give the glory to me."[6] Perhaps we should remember this association of the lyre with trickery, with lying words.

Athene is reputed to have invented the aulos but then to have quickly thrown it away when she discovered how ugly her face became while playing it. Marsyas (a satyr and thus a figure clearly related to Dionysos) found the discarded instrument and taught himself to play it. Indeed, he learned so well that he challenged Apollo to a contest to be judged by the Muses, a contest which the god—by cheating—won.

Orpheus's mother was one of these muses—not just any muse but Calliope, the one whose name means "beautiful voice," the one whom Hesiod named as the most exalted of them all. It was Calliope who thwarted Aphrodite by awarding Adonis to Persephone for a third of each year and the one who (in Ovid) gets to tell the Demeter-Persephone story and to tell it in a way that lays all the blame on Aphrodite.[7]

But that's to get far ahead. To begin with, Orpheus came from Thrace and he played the lyre. The earliest literary accounts mention his being a member of the Argonaut expedition (which makes him a contemporary of Herakles and of the other heroes of an age preceding the Trojan War). His primary assignment was to serve as the chanter who would keep the rowers in harmony with one another, but his beautiful singing was of much more help than that. First it coaxed the reluctant ship into the water and then at the very outset of the journey helped quell a brawl among the sailors. Later the ship was able safely to pass the Sirens as Orpheus' song drowned out theirs. It also charmed the Clashing Rocks, and even put the dragon in Colchis to sleep so that Jason could safely steal the golden fleece the fearsome beast was supposed to guard. Some of this is, of course, later elaboration, but already in the late archaic lyric poetry of Simonides we hear how Orpheus' singing had the power to charm wild beasts: "Above his head flutter innumerable birds and from the dark-blue sea fishes leap straight up in harmony with his lovely song."[8]

This is the Orpheus of the earliest visual art as well—Orpheus with his lyre, and the enchanted beasts. No underworld journey, no Eurydice, no dismemberment.

Then in the fifth century BCE we begin to hear of an underworld journey—as though the only challenge remaining to a poet who could charm the beasts would be to charm the powers that rule the underworld. Orpheus is now said to have gone to Hades to rescue an unnamed soul. This journey recalls Dionysos's journey to the underworld to rescue his mother Semele and bring her to Olympus, where as mother of a god, she to his mind rightfully belongs. Dionysos succeeds in his project and so, we surmise, did Orpheus in the earliest accounts. By virtue of his success Orpheus becomes someone believed to know the secrets of death and rebirth and to be able to teach them to others.

This version of Orpheus' descent is clearly influenced by the Orphic tradition in which Orpheus figures as a prophet of a Dionysos-centered eschatological mysticism. The Orphics probably were also the first to introduce the theme of dismemberment, a theme obviously echoing their myth about the dismemberment of Dionysos at the hands of the Titans. In the Orphic context dismemberment is understood as a ritual act associated both with vegetal fertility and with initiation. The death of Orpheus does not represent failure or punishment; it is the act whereby Orpheus fulfills his destiny.

A lost play by Aeschylus may have attributed the slaying of Orpheus to a band of Dionysian maenads angered at his rejection of their god for Apollo, and it evidently mentioned that he went to Hades "because of his wife" (the first known mention of this figure, though nothing more is said of her). But these are speculations about a vanished text; the first definite literary reference to an underworld descent undertaken as a rescue mission appears in Euripides' early play, *Alcestis*. In this early play after his wife's voluntary death, Admetus cries:

> Had I the lips of Orpheus and his melody
> to charm the maiden daughter of Demeter and
> her lord, and by singing win you back from death,
> I would have gone beneath the earth, and not the hound
> Of Pluto could have stayed me, nor the ferryman
> Of ghosts, Charon, at his oar, I would have brought you back
> To life.[9]

Yet despite this reference to an Orpheus who succeeded in his mission, the chorus (in its final song) says that it has nowhere found evidence of any power stronger than fate, neither Orpheus's songs nor Asclepius's healing potions. Thus the chorus sings of the hopelessness of victory over death—just before Herakles, through brute force, succeeds in bringing Alcestis back to the upperworld. So Euripides keeps the myth ambivalent: might Orpheus have succeeded or must he have failed? In his last or next to last play, *Iphigenia at Aulis* Iphigenia cries to Agamemnon: "If I had Orpheus' speech, my father…" But she knows she lives in a harsh real world where even a daughter's tears will have no power. So much for myths, she seems to say.

Initially the myth of Orpheus appears to celebrate art's power to triumph over death, an understanding that seems to be little more than an elaboration of the notion of poetry as power. But for there to be a real *story* about Orpheus he may need to suffer a genuine defeat, just as for there to be a *story* about Demeter and Persephone they need to suffer a separation. Unending success, unchallenged love, do not a story make. It may well be in Plato's *Symposium* that Orpheus is for the first time imagined as failing in his attempt. Failing because, so Phaedrus tells us, he didn't love enough, didn't love enough to die with the woman he had lost:

> Orpheus, son of Oeagros, they sent back unfulfilled from Hades, showing him a phantom of the woman for whom he came, but not giving the woman herself because he seemed to them to have acted the part of a coward since he was a singer with a lyre and didn't venture to die for the sake of love, as did Alcestis, but rather devised a means of entering Hades while still alive. Therefore they laid a just penalty upon him and caused his death to be at the hands of women.[10]

For Plato Orpheus failed in his mission—not because of a violated taboo, not because he'd been forbidden to look back upon his bride while returning her to the upperworld as in Virgil's or Ovid's versions—but because of a failure of character.

It is in the *Symposium* that for the first time Orpheus is imagined as going to rescue a particular beloved woman, though she still remains unnamed. Later in the fourth century BCE she gets a name: Ariope, which means "wild-voiced," a suitable name for a Thracian nymph or naiad. The name "Eurydice" does not appear until the first century BCE.[11]

In the Hellenistic period Orpheus comes to be associated with male homosexuality, a motif probably introduced to help explain his death at the hands of women.

So now the pieces of the myth are all there—for Virgil and Ovid to assemble, to re-member. It is still amazing to me that Virgil's masterfully condensed 75 lines in the *Georgics* (written around 29 BCE) should actually be the first narrative account of the myth. The Orpheus myth appears in Book 4 as an *epyllion*, a tale within a tale, a miniature epic. *Epyllia* were expected to recount an unfamiliar episode in the life of an important mythic figure. Because the frame and inset tales are expected to be thematically related, to understand Virgil's take on Orpheus we have to take account of the Aristaeus myth within which he sets it.

In Greek mythology Aristaeus is a son of Apollo (like Orpheus) and the sea nymph Cyrene, raised by Cheiron and tutored by the muses who taught him the arts of healing, prophecy, hunting and agriculture. He was also known as the father of Actaeon, cousin to Dionysos. Virgil invokes this familiar Aristaeus as a deity in the prologue to his poem; but in Book 4 he presents a new facet, here Aristaeus is a devoted beekeeper suddenly exposed to the inexplicable death of all his bees. Bewildered and dismayed, Aristaeus turns for help to his divine mother who advises him to consult Proteus, the ancient shapeshifting soothsaying seagod from whom he learns: "The anger that pursues you is divine" and can be traced to Orpheus' anguish at being separated from his wife. Proteus then proceeds to tell Aristaeus the full story: how Orpheus' wife, while fleeing from Aristaeus' unwanted embrace, had been bit by a death-bringing venomous serpent—and how this unnoticed, unremembered moment in Aristaeus' life has been pivotal in that of Orpheus.

Thus for Virgil the story of Orpheus begins with the death of his as yet unnamed wife, a wife who assumes an importance in this retelling she has never had before. Never before had there been an account of his wife's death—only of Orpheus's attempt to undo it. Never before had we had an account of Orpheus's grief, of his experience of her loss as unbearable. Virgil says that Orpheus tried without success to console himself with his own music:

> And you, sweet wife,
> You on the desolate shore alone he sang,
> You at return, you at decline of day.[12]

Unreconciled to his separation from Eurydice, Orpheus descends to the underworld, hoping to use his music to soften the hard hearts of Hades and Persephone. In a sense he is pulled into the underworld by his grief; the experience of loss *is* being there. But he hopes somehow to undo what has happened, to bring

Eurydice back to the land of the living. Virgil does not attempt to describe the poet's song, only how it drew all the too-early dead, the young mothers, the unwed virgins, the youths in fugitive bloom toward him, only how it struck with awe even the Furies and Cerberus and Ixion. Nor does Virgil make any direct reference to the gods' response. He only tells us that "having evaded every hazard," Orpheus was returning with Eurydice following close behind. Then suddenly "on the very brink of light" Orpheus forgets and "yielding in his will, looked back at his own Eurydice." Now, at this painful moment, just when she isn't "his," Eurydice is named for the first time. And only now are we, still indirectly, told of the taboo against looking back that has been violated. This, the prohibition against looking back and the consequent second loss, the very center of the myth as Virgil presents it, is almost surely his invention. And, of course, we know that things forbidden in such tales are always done (and suspect that maybe Hades and Persephone did as well). Orpheus is overcome by a *furor*, a madness of passion, which seizes him and turns him around.

Eurydice, now not only named, but given *voice*, subjectivity, is overwhelmed:

> 'Orpheus,' she cries, 'we are ruined, you and I!
> What utter madness is this? See, once again
> The cruel Fates are calling me back and darkness
> Falls on my swimming eyes. Goodbye for ever.
> I am borne away wrapped in an endless night,
> Stretching to you, no longer yours, these hands,
> These helpless hands.'

In Mary Zimmermann's beautiful enactment of this scene in her theatrical production "Metamorphoses" we watch Eurydice blindly following Orpheus until he turns and then we see the two lovers piteously, hopelessly, stretching out their hands, never quite touching, to one another. This happens once and it is almost unbearable. But then the whole scene is played out once again, and then a third time—as though maybe, maybe, the story might turn out differently. But, of course, it cannot—and we *feel* how this goodbye is, indeed, forever.

In Virgil's account it is Eurydice who speaks so plaintively; Orpheus is given no words except for one final plaintive, "Eurydice." As Eurydice finishes speaking, she vanishes like smoke, unable anymore to see Orpheus as he vainly grasps at shadows. Then back in the upperworld and powerless to return, Orpheus weeps for seven months, singing his tale of woe so movingly that tigers are entranced and oak trees draw close to listen, and wandering ever further north through a cold and barren landscape. Utterly consumed by his loss, Virgil's Orpheus in a sense never does really leave the underworld. Though forever separated from Eurydice, he can sing of nothing else, think of nothing else, feel nothing else. He is so deep *in* mourning—that his own death when it comes can only be release.

Virgil tell us of this death thus:

> Thracian women,
> Deeming themselves despised by such devotion
> Amid their Bacchic orgies in the night
> Tore him apart, this youth, and strewed his limbs
> Over the countryside.

This account (which reminds us of ancient rites in which a vegetation god is sacrificed) gives the death and the dismemberment a ritual context and significance. Orpheus who had at first refused to accept the necessity of nature's patterns of death and renewal now becomes a participant in a grim celebration of them. At the end of the framing tale Aristaeus (who is never shown feeling any remorse for his attempted rape) offers a sacrifice and is rewarded with the rebirth of his bees, an almost miraculous renewal of life. What Orpheus's sacrificial death accomplishes is more ambiguous. The river carries his severed head, still crying "Eurydice," down toward the sea; the riverbanks echo back, "Eurydice." What survives is this cry, this song, this name. And though Orpheus had once attempted to challenge nature's laws about the irrevocable character of human death, the oak-trees' sympathy, the river banks' echoing, suggest an ultimate harmony with the natural world. Nevertheless, Virgil's account is profoundly sad. There is no reunion, no release from suffering, separation, or death. And yet the poet in Virgil is also saying: But SONG is beautiful and it endures. Orpheus has given Eurydice a kind of immortality—her name still sounds—the kind that poets can confer (and Virgil has done the same for him). Art can't overcome death—but neither can death overcome art.

When Ovid comes to retell this story in Book 10 of his *Metamorphoses* Virgil's beautiful account serves as an inescapable model, one he can count on his audience knowing, and one against which he will explicitly be setting his own. He adds many details to Virgil's compact telling and in so doing changes the story—not its basic plot line, but its meaning. Ovid's version is more than ten times as long as Virgil's and there are losses as well as gains associated with the elaboration.

Ovid's telling of the Orpheus myth can be read as a deeply self-critical reflection on what it means to be a poet, and especially as a profound examination of what he takes to be the artist's inescapable narcissism. His own hubris is acknowledged in the very last word of his long poem: *Vivam* ("I shall live on").

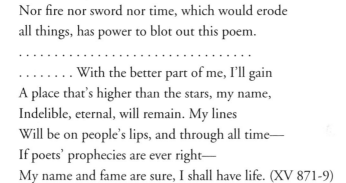

And now my work is done, no wrath of Jove
Nor fire nor sword nor time, which would erode
all things, has power to blot out this poem.
. . . .
. . . . With the better part of me, I'll gain
A place that's higher than the stars, my name,
Indelible, eternal, will remain. My lines
Will be on people's lips, and through all time—
If poets' prophecies are ever right—
My name and fame are sure, I shall have life. (XV 871-9)

We cannot help but smile at this narcissistic assurance—*and,* gratefully, acknowledge its truth.

It is through Ovid's consummately skillful complex design, through the way he uses juxtapositions, repetitions, subtle variations, the framing of tales within tales, subnarrators whom we have reason to regard with suspicion, that he suggests his interpretations. Orpheus is one of the most prominent of these subnarrators and it is in large measure through the stories he has Orpheus tell that Ovid conveys his understanding of Orpheus. And yet, even knowing that, we may find it difficult to be sure we know just what that understanding is. For there is an amazing degree of disagreement among good, careful scholars as to when Ovid is being serious, when playful; when judgmental, when sympathetic.

Ovid's telling of the myth begins with Hymen, the god of marriage, hastening to Thrace to be present at Orpheus's wedding but bringing no blessing—an ominous beginning. "The start was sad—and sadder still the end." (X.9) Almost immediately the bride, "just wed" (in Virgil Eurydice seems to be a long-loved wife) while in a meadow accompanied by nymphs, steps on a snake, is bit, and dies. The death is accidental, there is no Aristaeus, no attempted rape, no one to blame.

Unreconciled to his separation from Eurydice, Orpheus descends to the
underworld (some say more out of fascination with the role of bereaved lover
than out of true deep grief) and pleads with Persephone and Hades to restore
Eurydice to life. (Only now does Ovid introduce the name, as though only now
when lost does Eurydice begin to have an identity of her own rather than just that
of "bride," "my bride.") Ovid dares to give us the song that Orpheus sings in
hope of winning the dread gods' favor—though many readers believe that he has
deliberately put into Orpheus's mouth an artificial, highly rhetorical speech
devoid of true emotion. Perhaps Orpheus had never before sung so self-con-
sciously, with so desperate a hope that his song might once again have the magical power he had until now taken for granted.[13]

As I suggested above, it is hard, truly hard, to be sure we're reading Ovid ari-
ght. Perhaps it's best to say Ovid invites the questions, demands that we wonder:
Is Orpheus sincere or not? Does he love Eurydice or his own singing? Maybe
more important than arriving at an answer is getting that these are important
questions, that in a way both answers are true. For some of us, on some days, one
version may seem more compelling than the other—and that may tell us more
about ourselves than about Ovid or Orpheus. Ovid may help us realize that the
myth HOLDS these ambiguities—that that is what myths and archetypes do.
Ovid, I've come to believe, is deeply in touch with the tragedy *and the comedy* of
life.

On some days I find myself deeply moved by Orpheus reminding Persephone
and Hades of the love, which had long ago brought them together. I am ready to
trust Orpheus when he tells the underworld deities that he knows Eurydice must
eventually come under their rule, and assures them that if they won't agree to his
plea, he does not want to return to the upper world either. On other days I suspect that Ovid sees Orpheus as doing his best to flatter the gods, as putting forward his offer to stay in the underworld if necessary only as a persuasive rhetorical
motif.

As Orpheus continues his song even the Furies find their cheeks wet with
tears, Tantalus stops to listen to the poet's lament, the vultures desist from gnaw-
ing at Tityus's liver, and Sisyphus sits down on his rock—and Persephone and
Hades yield. They call Eurydice and she appears, still limping from her wound.
(Again, is this a touching detail or is it humorous?) In Ovid's version we learn of
the gods' command before Orpheus disobeys it. Here, too, he turns, but not
because possessed by a *furor*, but simply to make sure Eurydice is there and
because he longs to see her. It is not some overwhelming outside force but simply
Orpheus's own character that leads him to turn. This Eurydice makes no com-

plaint, but simply utters a faint "Farewell." Here his hands not hers reach out, and reach only "unresisting air." Here there is not quite the finality so inescapable in Virgil's telling; the bond between the two seems to remain unbroken, perhaps preparing us for the different ending Ovid will give his tale.

The second loss of Eurydice is in a sense the real loss, the irrevocable loss, though Orpheus is still not yet ready to accept that irreversibility. He tries to reenter Hades but Charon will not let him return. For Virgil seven painful months intervene between this second loss and Orpheus's own death. In Ovid Orpheus stays immobilized just outside Hades for seven days and then heads north and during the next three years, full of despair and anger over the loss of the woman he loved, repulses all the other women who desire him, and turns instead to the love of boys. For this Orpheus, despite his grief, life, it seems, goes on.

Like Virgil's Orpheus, Ovid's turns to his lyre to console himself. But where Virgil's can sing only his own tale of woe Ovid's says that he will "sing of boys whom the gods have loved and girls incited by unlawful lust." This sounds as though he sees himself as the one who has been betrayed, as though his loss is somehow Eurydice's fault, and as though this makes all women's love untrustworthy.

Actually, only Orpheus' first song, the one about Zeus and Ganymede, really fits his announced theme. As we look carefully at the stories he goes on to tell, we may sense that Orpheus himself does not fully understand how self-revealing they are: the love of gods and boys brings little joy to either; the females win our sympathy not our scorn. The stories suggest that loss and love seem to belong together, that the grief Orpheus has been exposed to is one that even the gods must suffer. There may also be hints of a not quite conscious sense of guilt; no, Orpheus was not responsible for Eurydice's first death, but it was his looking back that prevented her return, that kept her among the dead.

The second myth Orpheus retells focuses on Apollo's infatuation with the beautiful young huntsman Hyacinthus. While engaged in a discus-throwing competition, Apollo accidentally throws the discus so that rebounding it hits the youth full in the face and kills him. Even the healing god can do nothing. Overtaken by guilt and grief, he cries that he wishes that he might die for or with his beloved, but knows that as a god he can't but rather is doomed to grieve forever. "Your name shall always be upon my lips. The lyre my fingers pluck, the songs I chant, shall celebrate you." Obviously despite Orpheus's introduction, this is not a happy story: the god is exposed to the same kind of loss as Orpheus himself, and furthermore seems more aware of his own culpability.

Another of the longer songs focuses on the sculptor Pygmalion who is so "disgusted by the many sins to which the female mind had been inclined by nature," that he, like Orpheus, has completely turned away from women. Until, that is, he carves a stunningly beautiful and lifelike marble female figure with which he falls in love. He kisses it, caresses it, speaks to it, adorns it with jewels and beautiful clothes, gives it gifts, and imagines it coming to life. Eventually he prays to Aphrodite that this might really happen and she grants his prayer. Orpheus seems unaware of any connection between this artist who can only love the object he has himself created and his own love for the woman of his songs.

Orpheus also sings of Aphrodite's grief over the death of the mortal Adonis. She too has to learn how integrally love and loss are conjoined. He sings of Myrrh and her incestuous love for her father, and of Atalanta who had been warned by an oracle that if she were ever to yield to love she would lose herself. Both stories are told in a way that allows us to enter into the inner struggles of these women overtaken by passions, which overwhelm their conscious resolution.

As Orpheus sings his many songs, a whole grove of trees gathers close to give him shade and to listen. He sings so beautifully that savage beasts and even stones gather round and is so absorbed in his own singing that he fails to notice the approach of a band of threatening maenads.

Virgil speaks of these women as angered by Orpheus' unswerving devotion to Eurydice. In Ovid their describing him as "the man who dares to scorn us" is open to several alternative interpretations. Perhaps they act out of resentment of the misogyny they see evidenced in Orpheus's violent spurning of all women after Eurydice's loss. Or resentment of his having taught Thracian men the same same-sex preference? Or perhaps they are punishing him for a dedication to Apollo so intense as to imply a dishonoring of their god, Dionysos. They call him Apollo's poet; they drown out his lyre with their flutes, Dionysos' instrument. Or perhaps the maenads, women in touch with their own instinctual center, not defined by their roles as wives or mothers, represented that aspect of Eurydice which Orpheus who saw her only as *his* beloved had ignored: her in-herself-ness. This is close to Plato's view: Orpheus had never really loved Eurydice and for this, and the self-indulgence of his self-pity, the women kill him.

For when Orpheus tries to win these maenads over with his magical playing, he for the first time finds his song having no effect; it is drowned out by their cries and music. In Virgil the death has a ritual aspect; it happens as part of the women's "Bacchic rites;" there is even a sense of self-sacrifice implicit, as though Orpheus welcomes this death and as though it becomes part of a ritual renewal of life. In Ovid the maenads' killing seems more a rageful orgy of violence (with as usual some possibly comic overtones.) These maenads first direct their violence against all the birds and beasts that had allowed themselves to fall under Orpheus's spell, but this only serves to intensify their bloodthirstiness. Finding their stones inadequate they use their thrysi as spears, they start hurling clods of mud and ripped-off branches, they pick up shovels and hoes and use them as weapons. They murder Orpheus "in desecration" and engage in no ritual scattering of body parts.

But at the poet's death, all nature—the birds, the beasts, the very trees, even the streams and rivers—weeps. The severed head (and here the lyre as well) float down the river, murmuring mournfully. When the head comes to rest on the shores of Lesbos, it is attacked by a snake (as Eurydice had been so long ago) but Apollo intervenes to protect it and Dionysos, whose grief over the death of "Orpheus, the poet who had sung of Bacchus' sacred mysteries" was "great," intervenes to punish the maenads by turning them into trees.

The two gods whose protégé he is insure that after his death Orpheus will live on—as poet and as founder and prophet of the Orphic mysteries. His lyre is enshrined in a temple of Apollo—and thus Lesbos becomes the birthplace of lyric poetry. The head, buried under a temple of Dionysos, becomes the focus of an oracular hero-cult. This Orpheus, the Orpheus of the Orphics, is the singer of a theogony, which focuses on Dionysos as the man-god whose transcendence of death prefigures our own. Embodied life is seen as a burden from which after several lifetimes of ascetic discipline we might be freed. The afterlife is now seen as the real reality. Thus in this tradition Orpheus becomes one who leads us *into* the afterworld, rather than one who overcomes its claims or one destroyed by his refusal to accept them.

Ovid's version moves beyond the finality of Virgil's tragic ending; it is part of a *carmen perpetuum*—of a seamless song and a fluid world:

> The Shade of Orpheus
> Descends beneath the earth, The poet knows
> Each place that he had visited before;
> And searching through the fields of pious souls,
> He finds Eurydice.

Thus Orpheus, or rather his shade, now returns to the underworld, knowing it as he had not before, and is reunited with Eurydice. They greet each other with desirous arms, the "tender boys" evidently easily forgotten and forgiven. After his own death Orpheus is open to Eurydice's perspective as he had not been before.

When he returns to Hades, Orpheus and Eurydice are rejoined; now they walk together, each taking the lead in turn, and Orpheus may look back without risk upon his beloved.

The reunion brings together the shades, the souls, of Orpheus and Eurydice, and takes place in the underworld, the world of shades, phantoms, images. To put it another way: the reunion takes place, can only take place, in the imagination, in an *other* world.

It's as though Orpheus learned something from that earlier journey to the underworld after all, that it served as a kind of preparation for the later irreversible journey—and maybe his own songs served the same purpose. For our stories do often know more than we do. Orpheus may have begun his singing to divert himself from his grief and to express the anger aspect of his grief—but by telling stories that were not directly about himself, stories which enabled him to project his own experience onto others, he could begin to *see* his own (as his story may in turn help us see *ours).*

Orpheus had to learn about ends, had to learn that his relationship to Eurydice really was already over, that looking back was looking *back*, was a doomed attempt to keep the past intact. He had to learn that she is *herself,* not "his love."

For Eurydice, when regarded not as Orpheus' anima or muse but as herself, Hades may represent a kind of fulfillment. There is a poem of Rilke's called "Orpheus. Eurydice. Hermes." which long ago first made me aware of how different Eurydice's perspective on underworld experience may be from that of Orpheus. The poem is too long to quote in its entirety, but here are the lines which have impacted me most forcefully:

> But now she walked beside the graceful god,
> her steps constricted by the trailing graveclothes,
> uncertain, gentle, and without impatience.
> She was deep within herself, like a woman heavy
> with child, and did not see the man in front
> on the path ascending steeply into life.
> Deep within herself. Being dead
> filled her beyond fulfillment. Like a fruit
> suffused with its own mystery and sweetness,
> she was filled with her vast death, which was so new,
> she could not understand that it had happened.

She had come into a new virginity
and was untouchable; her sex had closed
like a young flower at nightfall, and her hands
had grown so unused to marriage that the god's
infinitely gentle touch of guidance
hurt her, like an undesired kiss.

She was no longer that woman with blue eyes
who once had echoed through the poet's songs,
no longer the wide couch's scent and island,
and that man's property no longer.

She was already loosened like long hair,
poured out like fallen rain,
shared like a limitless supply.

She was already root.

And when, abruptly,
the god put out his hand to stop her, saying,
with sorrow in his voice: He has turned around—,
she could not understand, and softly answered

       Who?[14]

From the perspective of Eurydice Hades looks, feels, *is* different. Perhaps we cannot even use the same words for underworld, cannot use the words that seem right from outside or even underway—but must instead turn words such as inwardness, cessation, peace. Rilke's Eurydice reminds me of my own period in the underworld and my resentment of would-be rescuers, who were irrelevant, were in the way—who didn't understand that this was *my* experience, that this was what I had now to live, that it had its own organic time which could not be foreshortened.

In herself Eurydice is a Persephone figure, one who belongs in the underworld as her name, *Eury-Dike*, makes clear. It means "broad ruling;" it suggests that she was originally an underworld goddess associated with the maintenance of a mode of natural order, of cosmic justice. Thus there are echoes in this tale of the old motif of the goddess and her lover-victim. Even in the myth as we have it, his love for her teaches him underworld realities—slowly. The initiation begins with *falling* in love, and then gradually learning what love means.

Eurydice like Persephone was brought to the underworld against her will, but then finds herself at home there, comes to embody its perspective, a perspective for which Orpheus was not yet ready. Again I turn to Rilke, to a much later poem, one of the *Sonnets to Orpheus*:

> Her sleep was everything.
>
> She slept the world. Singing god, how was that first
> sleep so perfect that she had no desire
> ever to wake?
>
> Where is her death now? Ah, will you discover
> this theme before your song consumes itself?[15]

For Rilke the myth is about Orpheus' discovery of his true theme. Though the song Orpheus sang to Persephone and Hades may still have been desire-driven, Orpheus ultimately means something else, something beyond desire which it took the first descent and its failure—once absorbed and understood—and his own death, to teach him:

> Song, as you have taught it, is not desire,
> . . . .
> True singing is a different breath, about
> nothing. (I, 3)

Rilke believed that a true poet's sole function was to bring the *Dinge,* the "things" of the world to word—not just to express his own feelings. Art is *transformation* not imitation of the natural world. This is what life is for: for poetry. *SINGING IS BEING.* And for him it is always Orpheus where there is song:

> We do not need to look
> for other names. Where there is poetry,
> it is Orpheus singing. (I.5)

The myth of Orpheus has also inspired many contemporary women poets, including H.D. of whom I spoke last year. Her "Eurydice," was written to express her angry disillusion over the discovery that for D. H. Lawrence (as earlier for Ezra Pound and for her husband Richard Aldington) she is more muse and desirable woman (though she wants to be that, too) than fellow poet (which she wants more than anything else). What most angers her is that Lawrence had aroused the hope that this time it might be different:

> So you have swept me back,
> I, who could have walked with the live souls
> Above the earth,
> I who could have slept among the live flowers
> At last;
>
> So for your arrogance
> And your ruthlessness
> I am swept back
> Where dead lichens drip
> Dead cinders upon moss of ash;
>
> So for your arrogance
> I am broken at last,
> I who had lived unconscious,
> Who was almost forgot;
>
> If you had let me wait
> I had grown from listlessness
> Into peace,
> If you had let me rest with the dead
> I had forgot you
> And the past.

Yet in the last lines of the poem H.D. reclaims her own passion and her own identity as a poet:

> At least I have the flowers of myself
> And my thoughts, no god

Can take that;
I have the fervour of myself for a presence
And my own spirit for light.[16]

Like H.D. my own way into the myth was through an identification with
Eurydice that led me to see in Orpheus primarily his inability to see her, to see
her as herself and not as his muse or anima (and to lay all the blame for this on
him, as though forgetting how tempting the role of anima-woman can be). But as
I have stayed engaged with the myth I've come to see it and him differently—as
Steve Kowit imagines Eurydice coming to see Orpheus differently during her
many solitary years in the underworld:

Truth to tell he was in many ways a child:
Impetuous, unthinking, willful in the way
A child is, who in his single-mindedness
& the immensity of his desire
cares nothing that the matter is impossible,
Am I to blame him for that one mistake?
. . . .
. . . . .Oh, who could
be so cruel that she would blame that boy.[17]

Eurydice need not stay where she was when she flung those last words at
Orpheus in Virgil's poem ("What utter madness")—remembering Orpheus need
not mean seeing him still as she saw him then. For remembering, as Freud wrote
in "Remembering, Repeating and Working-Through" is different from repeating; it is working-through, it is looking back with imagination so that something
new can be discovered. Orpheus's "looking back" when he hopes to return Eurydice to the upperworld is repetition; his "looking back" when he has rejoined her
in Hades, when he looks with what we might call "underworld eyes," with the
eyes of the soul, is re-membering.[18]

My own "looking-back" now also seems different from the "looking-back" of
fifteen years ago. For I now see that another way of understanding the story is to
see the death of Eurydice as representing the death of a projection, that is, as representing Orpheus's discovery that (to use Jungian terms) Eurydice was really an
anima figure and that it was now time to turn from her to a direct engagement
with the anima itself, with his own soul. So he went to the underworld, the world

where the soul lives. But because he went there to rescue the anima, to bring her back to the upperworld, he still hadn't really yet understood that the anima wasn't his; that the ego doesn't *have* an anima, that (as Hillman puts it) the point is not to develop my anima but to realize that anima-consciousness represents a way of being in the world.[19] It is only afterward, when he returns to the underworld to stay, that Orpheus comes to understand that he and Eurydice have to relate IN the underworld—that he has to look from the anima perspective not at it.

Once I saw this Orpheus, I of course saw that there are ways in which I am Orpheus and not just Eurydice; that the *myth* and not just this figure or that within it lives in me—and that looking at the story from a gendered perspective opens up some meanings and blinded me to others—as does adopting a Jungian perspective which might make Eurydice an anima figure for men and Orpheus an animus figure for women like me. I—not just "my animus"—AM Orpheus: his longing for depth, for connection, for love. But also his painful desperate wish that things might stay as they were—and his difficulty in recognizing that a beloved other truly is *other* and learning not only to accept that but bless it. Orpheus's guilt, his failures, his narcissistic delight in his own singing—all these are mine. As is the slow, slow learning that all his (and my) storying represents.

I think H.D. also came to see that she needed to recognize she was both Orpheus *and* Eurydice, poet and woman—or, perhaps more accurately stated, needed to learn how to get them *reconnected*. That need eventually brought her to Freud whom she experienced as midwife to the soul, as Asclepius the blameless physician, as the curator in a museum of priceless antiquities, as a trickster-thief nonchalantly unlocking vaults and caves, taking down the barriers that generations had carefully set up—and as an Orpheus who charms the very beasts of the unconscious and enlivens the dead sticks and stones of buried thoughts and memories[20]—a very different Orpheus from the one imagined in her early poem.

But Freud also helped her to discover that she—and not only—he was Orpheus.

> He was very beautiful,
> the old man,
> and I knew wisdom,
> I found measureless truth

in his words.

· · · · ·

he did not say
"stay,
be my disciple"—

· · · · · · ·

no,
he was rather casual,
"we won't argue about that"
(he said)
"you are a poet"[21]

She learned from him: You are a poet. You are Orpheus. You are Orpheus *and* Eurydice (as in the work we did on your big dream you were Moses *and* Miriam.)

And we, too—we, too—are Orpheus and Eurydice—and still, perhaps, not fully understanding all that that might mean.

Notes

1. Allen Mandelbaum, *The Metamorphoses of Ovid* (San Diego: Harcourt Brace, 1993) 361. Book XI, 64–66. All further quotations from Ovid will be from this translation indicated only by Book and line numbers.

2. Norman O. Brown, trans., *Hesiod: Theogony* (Indianapolis: Bobbs-Merrill, 1963) 53.

3. E. R. Dodds, *The Greeks and the Irrational* (Boston: Beacon, 1957) 147.

4. Or, in some versions, of a rivergod, Oeagros, who then turns out to be himself a descendent of Apollo.

5. W. K. C. Guthrie, *Orpheus and Greek Religion* (New York: Norton, 1966) passim.

6. Charles Boer, trans., "To Hermes," *The Homeric Hymns* (Chicago: Swallow Press, 1967) 22–61.

7. For the sake of consistency I have chosen to use the Greek names for the gods and goddesses even when Roman authors have used the Latin ones, except, of course, in direct quotation.

8. Quoted in Charles Segal, *Orpheus: The Myth of the Poet* (Baltimore: Johns Hopkins University Press, 1989) 13.

9. Richmond Lattimore, trans., "Alcestis," in David Grene and Richmond Lattimore, eds., *The Complete Greek Tragedies, Vol. III: Euripides* (Chicago: The University of Chicago Press, 1959) 20.

10. Michael Joyce, trans., in Edith Hamilton and Huntington Cairns, eds., *The Collected Dialogues of Plato* (Princeton: Princeton University Press, 1961) 533–534, 179.

11. Guthrie, 30.

12. L. Wilkinson, *Virgil: The Georgics* (New York: Penguin, 1982) 140, Book 4, 466–468. Further briefer quotes from the *Georgics* are from this same translation.

13. Paul Bresson, "Vicissitudes of Orpheus," *American Poetry Review,* May/June 1996, 19.

14. Mitchell, 51–53. I can't resist including part of a prose poem that Stephen Mitchell, Rilke's translator here, wrote imagining Persephone's response to Orpheus's plea:

   But this poor boy, this exquisite singer, will have a hard time ahead of him; she can tell by looking at his eyes. It is one thing to charm animals, trees, and rocks, and quite another to be in harmony with a woman. She recognizes his attitude, she has seen it before: fear protected by longing. Hence the bridal image, forever unattainable, forever ideal. No wonder Eurydice took the serpent's way out. Girls who are seen that way grow up to be maenads. If only, she thinks: If only there were some way to tell him. But, of course, he will have to learn for himself. To lose his love again and again, precipitously, as if by chance. To be torn in pieces, again and again.

   She turns to the king, "Yes, darling," she says, "Let him go." (Stephen Mitchell, "Orpheus," *Parables and Portraits* (New York: HarperCollins, 1994).

15. Stephen Mitchell, trans., "The Sonnets to Orpheus," *The Selected Poetry of Rainer Maria Rilke* (New York: Random House, 1982) 225, I, 2. All quotations from Rilke's Sonnets are from this translation, henceforth indicated only by number in the text.

16. H.D. "Eurydice," *Collected Poems 1912–1944* (New York: New Directions, 1983) 51–55.

17. Steve Kowit, "Eurydice," in Deborah Denicola, ed., *Orpheus and Company* (Hanover, NH: University Press of New England, 1999) 23–24.

18. Sigmund Freud, "Remembering, Repeating and Working-Through," *Standard Edition of the Complete Psychological Works of Sigmund Freud,* translated under the general editorship of James Strachey, Vol. XII (London: Hogarth Press, 1953–1974) 147–156.

19. James Hillman, "Anima," *Spring 1973,* 97–132.

20. H.D., *Tribute to Freud* (New York: McGraw-Hill, 1974) *passim.*

21. H.D., "The Master," *Collected Poems,* 451–452.

0-595-31086-9

Made in the USA
Coppell, TX
16 February 2020